Redouté's Roses
Redoutés Rosen
Les Roses de Redouté

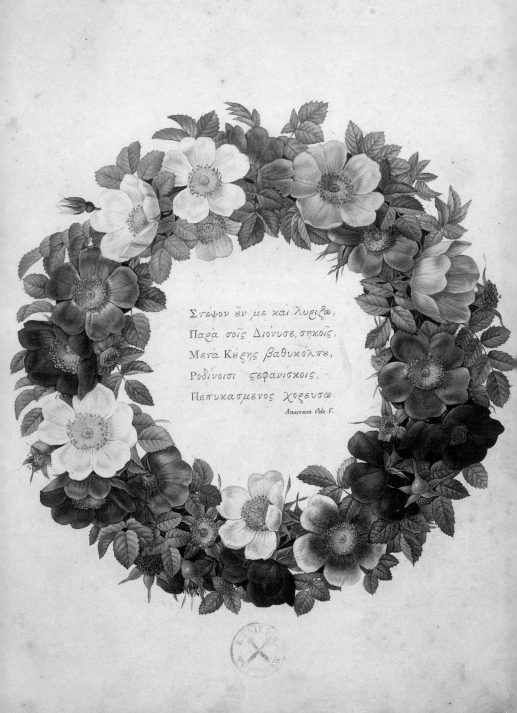

Στέφον ἂν με καὶ λυρίζω,
Παρὰ σοῖς Διόνυσε, σηκοῖς,
Μετὰ Κούρης βαθυκόλπε,
Ῥοδίνοισι ςεφανίσκοις,
Πεπυκασμένος χορεύσω.

Anacreon Ode V.

Redouté's Roses
Redoutés Rosen
Les Roses de Redouté

TASCHEN

KÖLN LONDON MADRID NEW YORK PARIS TOKYO

Acknowledgements | Danksagung | Remerciements

The copy used for printing belongs to the manuscript department of the university library in Erlangen-Nuremberg. We thank the library's employees for their friendly assistance.

Der Druck erfolgte nach dem Exemplar in der Universitäts-bibliothek Erlangen-Nürnberg, Handschriftenabteilung. Wir danken den Mitarbeitern der Bibliothek für die freundliche Unterstützung.

L'impression a été effectuée d'après l'exemplaire de la bibliothèque universitaire d'Erlangen-Nuremberg, département des manuscrits. Nous remercions le personnel de la bibliothèque pour son aimable soutien.

Photographs by Kurt Henseler, Tübingen
For the reproduction of the plates on pages 64, 68, 70, 71, 94, 108, 109, 113, 122, 123, 145 and 176 the volumes belonging to the manuscript department of the university library in Tübingen were used.
The reproduction of the plate on page 32 was made possible courtesy of the state library in Darmstadt.
© Archiv für Kunst und Geschichte, Berlin: ill. 8, 9

Front and back covers ROSA CHINENSIS JACQ. VAR. *SEMPERFLORENS* KOEHNE
'SLATER'S CRIMSON CHINA'
Monthly Rose 'Slater's Crimson China' (detail)

© 2001 TASCHEN GmbH, Hohenzollernring 53, D–50672 Köln
www.taschen.com
Editing Petra Lamers-Schütze, Cologne
Editorial coordination Christiane Blass, Susanne Klinkhamels, Cologne
Design Claudia Frey, Cologne
Production Thomas Grell, Cologne
English translation Harriet Horsfield in association with First Edition Translations Ltd., Cambridge, UK
French translation Annie Berthold, Düsseldorf
Printed in Italy
ISBN 3-8228-5554-5 [German]
ISBN 3-8228-1356-7 [English]
ISBN 3-8228-1355-9 [French]

Contents | Inhalt | Sommaire

Redouté and the

Redouté und die Kultur der Rose

Culture of Roses

Redouté et la culture des roses

PETRA-ANDREA HINZ

Pierre-Joseph Redouté was born on 10 July 1759 in St Hubert near Liège in an area of the Ardennes that is now in Belgium. He came from a family of painters. Churches and monasteries commissioned works from his grandfather, Jean-Jacques Redouté (1687–1752), and his father, Charles-Joseph Redouté (1715–1776) also earned his living as a painter. The three sons thus had an early introduction to art. Pierre-Joseph, however, was barely 15 years old when he left his father's care and, as was customary in those days, set out on his travels. He journeyed through Holland, Belgium and Luxembourg and accepted various commissions: interior decorations, portraits and religious works. He became familiar with the works of the great Flemish masters, particularly Rachel Ruysch (1664–1750) and Jan van Huysum (1682–1749)

In 1782, Pierre-Joseph Redouté went to Paris, where the Dutchman Gerard van Spaendonck (1746–1822) introduced him to iconography of the natural world, which led to his appointment as scientific draftsman at the museum. During his time at the Jardin du Roi, Pierre-Joseph Redouté came

Pierre Joseph Redouté wurde am 10. Juli 1759 in St. Hubert in der Nähe von Lüttich in den belgischen Ardennen geboren. Er stammte aus einer Familie von Malern; sein Großvater Jean-Jacques Redouté (1687–1752) arbeitete im Auftrag für Kirchen und Klöster, und auch sein Vater Charles-Joseph Redouté (1715–1776) verdiente seinen Lebensunterhalt als Maler. So wurden die drei Söhne vom Vater in die Kunst eingeführt. Mit kaum 15 Jahren war Pierre-Joseph der väterlichen Obhut entwachsen und begab sich, wie damals üblich, auf Wanderschaft. Er zog durch Holland, Belgien und Luxemburg und nahm verschiedene Aufträge an: Innendekorationen, Porträts und religiöse Themen. Er lernte die Werke der großen flämischen Meister kennen, besonders Rachel Ruysch (1664–1750) und Jan van Huysum (1682–1749).

1782 ging Pierre-Joseph Redouté nach Paris, wurde von dem Holländer Gerard von Spaendonck (1746–1822) in die naturkundliche Ikonographie eingeführt und erhielt eine Anstellung als wissenschaft-

Pierre-Joseph Redouté est né le 10 juillet 1759 à Saint-Hubert, près de Liège, en Belgique. Il est issu d'une famille de peintres. Son grand-père Jean-Jacques Redouté (1687–1752) et son père Charles-Joseph Redouté (1715–1776) ont travaillé pour divers monastères et abbayes. Les trois fils reçurent tout jeunes l'enseignement du père. A l'âge de quinze ans à peine, Pierre-Joseph quitta l'atelier paternel pour parfaire sa formation, comme cela se faisait à l'époque. Au cours de ses pérégrinations en Hollande, en Belgique et au Luxembourg, il réalisa divers travaux de décoration, portraits et peintures religieuses. Il découvrit les œuvres des grands peintres flamands ainsi que les productions des peintres de fleurs comme Rachel Ruysch (1664–1750) et Jan van Huysum (1682–1749).

En 1782, Pierre-Joseph Redouté se rendit à Paris et fit la connaissance du Hollandais Gerard van Spaendonck (1746–1822) le familiarisa avec l'iconographie didactique. Il obtient ensuite un

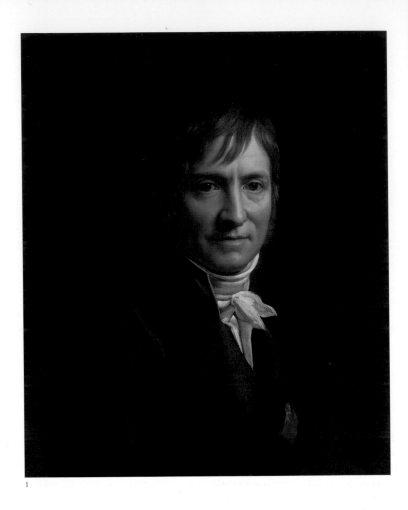

1

1 │ BARON FRANÇOIS GÉRARD
Pierre-Joseph Redouté (1759–1840)
Bruxelles, Musées royaux des Beaux-Arts de Belgique

to know the wealthy amateur botanist, Charles-Louis L'Héritier de Brutelle (1746–1800). While looking for a suitable illustrator for his works, he noticed the young Redouté and recognised his great talent. L'Héritier instructed Redouté in plant anatomy, showed him the morphologically important characteristics of the plants and allowed him to use his large private library. On the basis of the botanical knowledge he acquired from L'Héritier, Redouté was able for the first time to make his pictures scientifically exact.

In 1787, Redouté came with L'Héritier to London. While there, he also learnt about single-plate colour printing, which, unlike the French colour engraving process that requires three or four plates, uses only one plate with several colours.

Redouté's most important creative period began when, in 1798/99, Napoleon's first wife, Joséphine, acquired the Malmaison château in Rueil, west of Paris.

licher Zeichner am Museum des Jardin du Roi. Während seiner Zeit am Jardin du Roi lernte Pierre-Joseph Redouté den wohlhabenden Amateurbotaniker Charles-Louis L'Héritier de Brutelle (1746–1800) kennen. Auf der Suche nach einem geeigneten Illustrator für seine Werke fiel ihm der junge Redouté auf, und er erkannte dessen großes Talent. L'Héritier unterwies Redouté in der Anatomie der Pflanzen, zeigte ihm ihre morphologisch wichtigen Merkmale und öffnete ihm seine große Privatbibliothek. Aufgrund der von L'Héritier erworbenen botanischen Kenntnisse konnte Redouté erst die wissenschaftliche Genauigkeit seiner Darstellungen erreichen.

1787 kam Redouté in Begleitung von L'Héritier nach London. Er lernte dort den Einplattenfarbdruck kennen, der im Gegensatz zum französischen Farbstichverfahren mit drei bis vier Platten nur eine, allerdings mehrfarbig eingefärbte Platte benutzte.

Redoutés wichtigste Schaffensperiode begann, als Napoleons erste Gattin, die spätere Kaiserin Josephine,

poste de dessinateur scientifique au Musée du Jardin du Roi.

Durant son travail au Jardin du Roi, Pierre-Joseph Redouté fit la connaissance de Charles-Louis L'Héritier de Brutelle (1746–1800), riche botaniste amateur. Recherchant un bon illustrateur, celui-ci remarqua le jeune Redouté et reconnut son talent. L'Héritier lui révéla l'anatomie des végétaux, leurs caractéristiques morphologiques, et lui ouvrit sa riche bibliothèque privée. Redouté n'a pu parvenir à la précision scientifique qui caractérise ses illustrations que grâce à l'enseignement de L'Héritier.

En 1787, Redouté se rendit à Londres en compagnie de L'Héritier. Il découvrit une nouvelle technique d'impression en couleur : à la différence du procédé français de l'impression polychrome par passage de trois ou quatre plaques, on n'utilisait qu'une seule plaque pour plusieurs couleurs.

La période la plus féconde de Redouté commence en 1798–99, lorsque la femme de Napo-

Thanks to the Empress it was made possible to build up a collection, unique at that time, of plants from outside Europe in just a few years at Malmaison. Joséphine's aim, however, was not just to lay out a beautiful garden, but also to cultivate the collected varieties scientifically. This gave rise to a magnificent, large format work, *Jardin de Malmaison* (1803–1805), with 120 plates from watercolours by Redouté.

Under the patronage of Empress Joséphine, the book on *Liliaceae* was also published from 1802 to 1816 in several volumes. With 486 colour engravings, all produced from Redoutés own watercolours, the title *Les Liliacées* is his most comprehensive work.

Joséphine's special interest, however, was roses. She was in constant contact with the most important European rose growers and breeders and had a rose garden laid out with the intention of growing all known varieties of rose there. When Empress Joséphine died in 1814, the garden contained around 250 rose varieties.

im Jahre 1798/99 die Grafschaft Malmaison in Rueil, westlich von Paris, erwarb.

Unter ihr entstand in wenigen Jahren in Malmaison eine zu jener Zeit einmalige Sammlung außereuropäischer Pflanzen. Josephines Ziel war aber nicht nur die Anlage eines schönen Gartens, sondern auch die wissenschaftliche Bearbeitung der zusammengetragenen Arten. Es entstand ein großformatiges Prachtwerk Jardin de Malmaison (1803–1805) mit 120 Tafeln nach Aquarellen von Redouté.

Redouté arbeitete gleichzeitig an dem mehrbändigen Werk Les Liliacées, das 1802–1816 unter dem Protektorat der Kaiserin Josephine publiziert wurde. Mit 486 Farbpunktstichen, die alle nach Redoutés eigenen Aquarellen hergestellt wurden, ist das Lilienwerk das umfangreichste Werk Redoutés.

Das besondere Interesse Josephines aber galt den Rosen. Sie pflegte ständigen Kontakt mit den bedeutendsten europäischen Rosengärtnereien sowie Baumschulen und ließ einen Rosengarten anlegen, in dem alle

léon, la future impératrice Joséphine, achète le château de Malmaison près du village de Rueil, à l'ouest de Paris. Grâce à l'impératrice, Malmaison réunit en quelques années une extraordinaire collection de plantes non-européennes, unique à l'époque. Mais Joséphine ne voulait pas qu'aménager un beau jardin, son intention était aussi de faire une étude scientifique de la collection. Ces études furent réunies en un magnifique recueil, le Jardin de Malmaison (1803–1805), avec 120 planches exécutées à l'aquarelle par Redouté.

Redouté travailla en parallèle sur l'édition en plusieurs volumes des Liliacées publiés sous le patronnage de l'impératrice. Avec 486 planches en couleurs, toutes exécutées d'après les aquarelles de Redouté, Les Liliacées constitue l'œuvre la plus considérable de l'artiste.

Mais Joséphine avait une prédilection pour les rosiers. Elle était en contact avec les plus grands rosiéristes d'Europe et se fit planter une roseraie où

The three volumes of Redouté's rose book were published in 30 installments between 1817 and 1824. There was a large folio edition of only five copies, which contained a monochrome engraving and a hand-coloured engraving for each rose. The small folio edition was printed at the same time. Redouté's rose monograph also enjoyed immediate success and had to be reprinted shortly after it first appeared.

Redouté survived the difficult years of the Revolution and the Restoration and found approval with the all the rulers who changed in quick succession. Redouté illustrated approximately 50 botanical books, but did not, however, publish any plant descriptions himself. Nor did he create a herbarium. A few examples from the Malmaison garden that served as subjects for his drawings can still be found in Paris today. He died on 20 June 1840, almost 81 years old, and was buried at the Père Lachaise cemetery in Paris.

bekannten Sorten wachsen sollten. Bis zu ihrem Tod 1814 waren hier rund 250 Rosensorten angesiedelt.

Die drei Rosenbände von Redouté enthalten 170 Tafeln und wurden in 30 Teillieferungen 1817–1824 veröffentlicht. Eine große Folio-Ausgabe erschien zunächst in nur 5 Exemplaren und enthielt für jede Rose einen unkolorierten Stich und einen von Hand kolorierten Farbstich. Gleichzeitig wurde eine kleine Folio-Ausgabe herausgegeben. Das Werk hatte großen Erfolg und wurde bereits kurz nach Erscheinen nachgedruckt.

Redouté überlebte die schwierigen Jahre der Revolution und der Restauration und fand Anerkennung bei den rasch wechselnden Machthabern. Er illustrierte nahezu fünfzig botanische Bücher, veröffentlichte jedoch selbst keine Pflanzenbeschreibungen und legte auch kein Herbarium an. Einige Belege aus dem Garten von Malmaison, die als Vorlage für seine Zeichnungen dienten, befinden sich heute in Paris. Er starb am 20. Juni 1840, fast 81 Jahre alt, und wurde auf dem Friedhof Père Lachaise in Paris beigesetzt.

elle voulait faire pousser tous les rosiers connus. Jusqu'à sa mort en 1814, 250 espèces y furent cultivées.

La publication des trois volumes de Redouté se fit de 1817 à 1824, en 30 livraisons partielles et tirage simultané en deux formats : un grand in-folio qui parut en 5 exemplaires seulement, avec pour chaque rosier une planche coloriée et une planche non coloriée, et un petit in-folio. La monographie de Redouté eut un tel succès qu'il fallut la réimprimer sitôt après la première parution.

Redouté survécut à la Révolution et à la Restauration et fut en faveur auprès de tous les dirigeants qui se sont succédé au pouvoir. Si Redouté a illustré cinquante livres environ, il n'a rédigé lui même aucune description de végétaux et ne s'est jamais confectionné d'herbier. Quelques échantillons de plantes qui lui ont servi de modèles pour ses dessins se trouvent aujourd'hui à Paris. Redouté mourut le 20 juin 1840 à l'âge de 81 ans et fut enterré au cimetière parisien du Père-Lachaise.

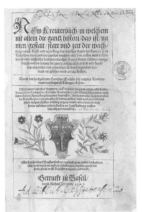

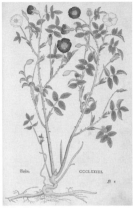

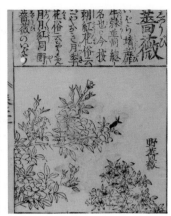

2   3   4

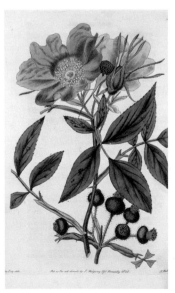

2 | LEONHART FUCHS: NEW KREÜTERBUCH, 1543
  Eichstätt, Seminarbibliothek

3 | LEONHART FUCHS: NEW KREÜTERBUCH, 1543
  CCCLXXIIII: Rosa gallica
  Eichstätt, Seminarbibliothek

4 | TEKISAI NAKAMURA: KINMOZUI, 1668
  Ibara
  Munich, Staatsbibliothek

5 | JOHN LINDLEY: ROSARUM MONOGRAPHIA, 1820
  Rosa carolina L.
  London, Natural History Museum

5

THE ROSE GENUS

Depending on the opinion of different authors, the genus Rosa L. comprises one hundred to two hundred species. It is very difficult to identify a species, and here expert botanical opinion often varies widely, since the species are very variable and hybridise easily, meaning that many hybrids arise naturally.

Roses are mainly deciduous, rarely evergreen, erect or climbing shrubs, in other words they produce several shoots from the base, which produce further side shoots. The branches are more or less bristly and prickly. These prickles are sharp, pointed outgrowths of the bark tissue, which is why, unlike true thorns, they are easy to break off. They act as holdfasts and are very important for the reliable identification of a species. Other forms of weaponry are soft, flexible spiny bristles, glandular bristles, which have a spherical gland at their tip, and stem glands. The leaves are alternate, imparipinnate, in other words they have a terminal partial leaf

DIE GATTUNG DER ROSEN

Die Gattung Rosa L. umfaßt hundert bis zweihundert Arten, je nach Auffassung der Autoren. Die Abgrenzung der Arten, über die die Meinungen der Botaniker oft weit auseinandergehen, ist sehr schwierig, da die Arten sehr variabel sind und leicht hybridisieren, das heißt, sich leicht kreuzen.

Rosen sind sommergrüne, seltener immergrüne, aufrechte oder kletternde Sträucher. Sie haben natürlicherweise nicht nur einen Stamm, sondern mehrere Sproßachsen, die sich in mittlerer Höhe verzweigen. Ihre Triebe sind meist mehr oder weniger stachelig und borstig. Diese Stacheln sind spitze, stechende Auswüchse des Rindengewebes, weshalb sie im Gegensatz zu Dornen leicht abzubrechen sind. Sie dienen als Haftorgane und sind zur sicheren Bestimmung einer Art sehr wichtig. Weitere Formen der Bewehrung sind weiche, biegsame Stachelborsten, Drüsenborsten, die an ihrer Spitze eine kugelige Drüse haben, und Stieldrüsen. Die Blätter sind wechselständig, unpaarig gefiedert, das heißt, sie tragen ein

LE GENRE ROSA

Selon les auteurs, le genre Rosa L. compte cent à deux cents espèces. La distinction – une question sur laquelle divergent souvent les avis des botanistes –, s'avère peu aisée car les rosiers sont sujets à des mutations et s'hybrident facilement. Les rosiers sont des arbustes à feuillage caduc, rarement persistant, au port droit ou grimpant, ce qui signifie qu'ils n'ont pas seulement un tronc, mais plusieurs axes se ramifiant à mi-hauteur. Les tiges sont normalement munies d'aiguillons et de poils raides. Les aiguillons sont des piquants pointus, parfois recourbés, formés à partir des tissus épidermiques de la tige, c'est pourquoi ils sont plus faciles à casser que les épines. Ils servent d'organe d'adhérence et sont importants pour la détermination d'une espèce. L'armement peut prendre d'autres formes : poils souples en crochet, poils glanduleux – les glandes rondes se situent à l'extrémité des poils – et glandes pédonculées. Les feuilles sont

and auxiliary leaves. The leaves are rarely simple, as is the case with the Persian rose, for example. The auxiliary leaves are small, leaf-like structures on each side of the leaf base and are usually attached to the leaf stalk. The flowers are solitary or borne in corymbs at the ends of short lateral branches. The inflorescences of wild or species roses are arranged singly, in threes or very occasionally in fives. Garden roses can bear large clusters or panicles of flowers with up to a hundred blooms on one stem. Each individual flower has five sepals, five petals, numerous stamens and many pistils. Modification of the stamens and pistil into petal-like structures produces double-flowered garden roses. Garden roses with five to ten petals are defined as single; those with ten to twenty petals are considered to be semi-double; and those with more than twenty petals are referred to as fully double. The calyx is an elongated structure that unites the ovary and the other reproductive organs. The individual sepals display characteristics that make it easy to identify a species or variety. It is not only their shape (for example simple or

endständiges Teilblatt und Nebenblätter. Selten sind die Blätter einfach, wie zum Beispiel bei der Persischen Rose. Die Nebenblätter bilden kleine blattartige Gebilde zu beiden Seiten der Blattbasis und sind meist mit dem Blattstiel verwachsen. Die Blüten stehen einzeln oder in Doldenrispen an den Enden kurzer Seitenzweige. Wildrosen haben ein- bis dreiblütige, seltener fünfblütige Blütenstände, Gartenrosen können große traubige oder rispige Blütenstände mit bis zu hundert Blüten an einem Trieb tragen. Eine einzelne Blüte hat natürlicherweise fünf Kelch-, fünf Kron-, zahlreiche Staubblätter und viele Stempel. Gefüllte Gartenformen entstehen durch Umwandlung von Staubblättern und Griffeln zu kronblattartigen Gebilden. Gartenrosen mit fünf bis zehn Kronblättern werden noch als einfach bezeichnet, solche mit zehn bis zwanzig Kronblättern gelten als halbgefüllt und solche mit mehr als zwanzig Kronblättern als gefüllt.

Der Kelch, genauer gesagt der Kelchbecher, ist ein relativ langes, röhriges Achsenstück zwischen dem

alternes, pennées, c'est-à-dire composées de plus de trois folioles disposées par paires de part et d'autre d'un axe commun, avec une foliole terminale, et munies d'un stipule. Rares sont les feuilles simples, comme par exemple dans le rosier de Perse. Le stipule est un appendice en forme de feuille, situé à la base du pétiole et généralement soudé à celui-ci. Les fleurs sont solitaires ou en panicules au bout de courts pédoncules. Les rosiers sauvages ont des inflorescences ornées d'une à trois fleurs, rarement cinq; les rosiers de jardin peuvent fleurir en grosses grappes ou en panicules et porter jusqu'à cent fleurs par tige. La fleur a généralement cinq sépales et cinq pétales; les étamines et les pistils sont nombreux. Les fleurs doubles qui fleurissent sur certains rosiers de jardin sont dues à une modification des étamines et des pistils. Les fleurs simples sont formées de cinq à dix pétales, les fleurs semi-doubles ont de dix à vingt pétales, et les fleurs doubles, plus de vingt. Le calice, tubulé, est placé

pinnatifid) and their size (especially in relation to the petals) which are important, but also how long they persist while the fruit ripens and their position (erect or arched downwards). The five petals of the wild roses are usually broadly rounded, rounded or broadly oval. At the base they have a small attachment, known botanically as a claw. The upper edge of the petals can be rounded or roughly heart-shaped, as can be seen on many of Redouté's illustrations. The flower colour varies from white through pink to red. In Asia, there are even some yellow wild species. Blue does not occur. The fruit develops from the receptacle and is commonly known as a rose hip. The genus can be further divided into two sub-genera: subgenus *Hulthemia* Focke is distinguished by simple leaves with no auxiliary leaves, and single erect yellow flowers, cf. *Rosa persica* Michaux; subgenus *Eurosa* Focke includes the more usual roses with pinnate leaves bearing auxiliary leaves. It is not easy to classify the individual rose groups, including wild species roses, and complete empirical evidence is required to do so.

Fruchtknoten und den übrigen Blütenorganen. Die einzelnen Kelchblätter weisen Merkmale auf, die das Identifizieren einer Art oder Sorte erleichtern. Zur Bestimmung ist aber nicht nur ihre Form (zum Beispiel einfach oder fiederspaltig) und ihre Größe (vor allem im Verhältnis zu den Kronblättern) wichtig, sondern auch ihre Dauer während der Fruchtreife und ihre Stellung (aufgerichtet oder nach unten gebogen). Die fünf Blütenblätter der Wildrosen sind meist breitrund, rund oder breit verkehrteiförmig, an der Basis haben sie eine kleine Ansatzstelle, die in der Botanik Nagel genannt wird. Der obere Rand der Blütenblätter kann rund oder mehr oder weniger herzförmig eingeschnitten sein, so wie es auf vielen Darstellungen Redoutés zu erkennen ist. Die Blütenfarbe variiert von Weiß über Rosa zu Rot, in Asien treten auch gelbblütige Wildarten auf. Blau kommt in der Natur nicht vor. Die Frucht bildet sich aus dem Kelchbecher, sie wird allgemein Hagebutte genannt.

Eine wichtige Unterteilung der Gattung ist die Unterscheidung von zwei Untergattungen: Subgenus

entre l'ovaire et les autres organes floraux. Les sépales ont des caractéristiques propres qui facilitent l'identification d'une espèce ou d'une variété. Non seulement leur forme (simple ou divisée, par exemple), mais leur grandeur (en particulier, par rapport aux pétales), leur durée à maturité ainsi que leur port (droit ou courbé) sont également importants pour l'identification. Les rosiers sauvages, appelés aussi rosiers botaniques, ont cinq pétales, le plus souvent largement ronds, ronds ou largement ovales ; à leur base se trouve une petite excroissance de tissus membraneux, appelée ligule. Les pétales peuvent être arrondis ou légèrement échancrés au sommet, ainsi qu'on le voit sur de nombreuses illustrations de Redouté. Les coloris vont du blanc au rouge en passant par le rose. En Asie, certains rosiers sauvages sont de couleur jaune. Il n'existe, en revanche, aucune rose bleue. Le fruit de la rose ou cynorrhodon, appelé communément gratte-cul, se développe à partir du calice.

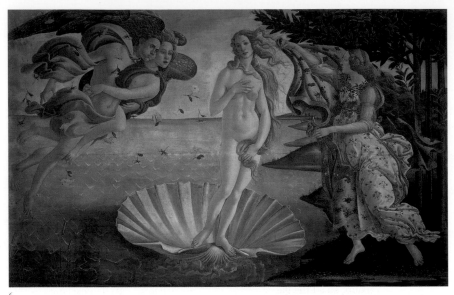

6

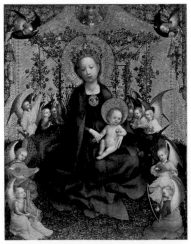

6 | SANDRO BOTTICELLI (1445–1510)
The Birth of Venus, c. 1485
Geburt der Venus, um 1485
Naissance de Vénus, vers 1485
Florence, Galleria degli Uffizi

7 | STEFAN LOCHNER (1405/15–1451)
Madonna in the Rose Bower, c. 1450
Muttergottes in der Rosenlaube, um 1450
Madone à la roseraie, vers 1450
Cologne, Wallraf-Richartz-Museum

7

GARDEN ROSES

Unlike the wild roses, garden roses are developed by man and not by nature. They are a product of controlled breeding and are given variety or cultivar names. A variety describes a stock of cultivated plants that has particular distinguishing features that it retains when propagated vegetatively. To make it easier to get an overview, the huge number of rose varieties are divided into different groups, but today, reflecting the huge gene pool of roses, they are also divided into "old garden roses", "modern garden roses" and the wild roses described above. Each group includes climbing and bush roses.

A rose is described as an "old rose" if it belongs to a rose category (in the horticultural sense) that was in existence prior to 1867. The first crosses with the Asiatic species introduced in the 19th century still come under this group, so all the garden roses drawn by Redouté can be described as "old roses". The phrase "modern roses" was not used until 1867, when the first

Hulthemia *Focke zeichnet sich durch einfache Blätter, ohne Nebenblätter und einzeln stehende gelbe Blüten aus, vgl.* Rosa persica *Michaux; Subgenus* Eurosa *Focke schließt die typischen Rosen mit gefiederten, Nebenblätter tragenden Blättern ein. Die schwierige Bestimmung der einzelnen Rosenarten, auch der Wildarten erfordert ein vollständiges Untersuchungsmaterial.*

ROSEN IN DER GARTENKULTUR

Im Gegensatz zu den Wildrosen sind die Gartenrosen von Menschenhand und nicht von der Natur geformt, sie stellen ein gärtnerisches Züchtungsprodukt dar und werden zu Sorten oder Cultivaren zusammengefaßt. Als Sorte bezeichnet man einen Bestand kultivierter Pflanzen, der sich durch besondere Merkmale auszeichnet und bei der Fortpflanzung seine sortentypischen Merkmale beibehält. Die Vielzahl der Rosensorten wird der besseren Übersicht halber in sogenannte Klassen eingeteilt, aber heute sind aufgrund der starken züchterischen Vermischung des Erbgutes der Rosen auch die übergeord-

Le genre se divise en deux sous-genres :
Subgenus *Hulthemia* Focke se caractérise par des feuilles simples, sans stipules, et des fleurs solitaires jaunes, comme *Rosa persica* Michaux; Subgenus *Eurosa* Focke comprend les roses typiques, à feuilles pennées et stipulées.

LES ROSIERS DANS L'HISTOIRE HORTICOLE

A la différence des rosiers sauvages, les rosiers cultivés sont une pure création de l'homme. Ils constituent des variétés ou « cultivars ». Par variété, on entend une population de plantes cultivées qui présente des signes distinctifs et conserve ses caractères types à la fécondation. Les variétés de rosiers, du fait de leur nombre impressionnant, sont classées en diverses catégories, mais leur capital génétique respectif étant devenu indistinct par suite de croisements répétés, on fait maintenant la différence entre « rosiers anciens », « rosiers modernes »

18

hybrid tea (large-flowered bush) roses were introduced. In this connection, the lifespan of a rose variety is also significant, in the sense of how long the variety is available on the market. As a general rule, this is not for long, although many of the old roses are already more than 150 years old. They would have died out long ago had not rose growers and enthusiasts continued to cultivate them despite their faults, such as their short flowering period, for example. Nowadays, most rose varieties are on the market for little more than five years before they are replaced by newer, improved varieties.

As cultivated plants, rose varieties are now given names on three main levels: genus, species and variety (cultivar), with variety being the lowest level. The genus and species names are in Latin, while modern languages are used for the variety names, which are shown in single quotation marks ('…').

nete Einteilung der Rosen in »Alte Gartenrosen«, »Moderne Gartenrosen« und die oben vorgestellten Wildrosen von Bedeutung. Innerhalb jeder Gruppe wird zwischen kletternden und nicht kletternden Rosen unterschieden.

Eine Rose wird als »Alte Rose« bezeichnet, wenn sie zu einer Rosenklasse im gärtnerischen Sinne gehört, die bereits vor 1867 bestand. Die ersten Züchtungen mit den im 19. Jahrhundert eingeführten asiatischen Arten gehören noch zu dieser Gruppe, somit sind alle von Redouté gezeichneten Gartenrosen als »Alte Rosen« zu bezeichnen. Erst mit der Einführung der ersten Teehybride 1867 spricht man von »Modernen Rosen«. In diesem Zusammenhang ist die Lebensdauer einer Rosensorte auch beachtenswert, das heißt, die Zeitspanne während der die Sorte im Handel angeboten wird. Sie ist im allgemeinen relativ kurz, nur die Alten Rosen sind oft schon über 150 Jahre alt. Sie wären längst ausgestorben, wenn nicht Rosarien und Liebhaber ihren Anbau trotz ihrer Schwächen, wie beispielsweise ihre kurze Blütezeit, pflegen würden. Heute bleiben die meisten

et « rosiers sauvages ou botaniques ». De plus, à l'intérieur de chaque groupe, on distingue entre rosiers grimpants et rosiers non grimpants.

Un rosier est « ancien » lorsqu'il appartient à une classe qui existait avant 1867. Les premiers hybrides font partie de ce groupe. Par conséquent, toutes les roses de jardin dessinées par Redouté sont « anciennes ». C'est avec la création du premier hybride de Thé, en 1867, qu'on a commencé à parler de « rosier moderne ». La durée de vie d'un rosier, c'est-à-dire sa période de commercialisation, est un autre facteur important. Elle est plutôt courte pour un rosier moderne, alors que les rosiers anciens existent souvent depuis plus de 150 ans. Ils auraient disparu, si rosiéristes et amateurs ne continuaient à les cultiver en dépit de leurs faiblesses (floraison éphémère par exemple). De nos jours, la plupart des variétés restent à peine plus de cinq ans sur le marché, jusqu'à l'apparition de créations de meilleure qualité. Le nom botanique des

ROSE SCENT

Since the Ancient Greek and Roman times, people have tried to capture the scent of rose flowers in a usable form. Perfumed ointments were produced by extracting the oils and fats from rose petals. However, it was not possible to isolate the pure essential oil until the Arabs had invented steam distillation. Today, a variety of the damask rose (*Rosa × damascena* Miller 'Trigintipetala') is the most important rose for oil production. Around 1700, the Turks introduced oil rose cultivation to the Balkans, but it spread only to the "Valley of the Roses" in northern Thrace in Bulgaria. Production of "Bulgarian rose oil" in the Anatolian Mountains of Turkey has now outstripped that of its country of origin. At a height of 1000 m, the ecological conditions are particularly favourable for growing damask roses. Bulgarian rose oil is used not only in pharmacology and medicine, but also in the perfume and cosmetics industries. In southern France and Morocco, an essential oil is produced from the Provence rose by means of steam distillation. It

Rosensorten kaum länger als fünf Jahre im Handel, bis sie von neueren, verbesserten Sorten verdrängt werden.

Als Kulturpflanzen erhalten die Rosensorten heute Namen auf drei Hauptrangstufen: Gattung, Art und Sorte (Cultivar), wobei Sorte die niedrigste Rangstufe darstellt. Während Gattungs- und Artnamen latinisiert werden, sollen Sortennamen lebenden Sprachen entnommen werden. Sie werden in einfache Anführungszeichen ('...') gesetzt.

ROSENDUFT

Seit der Antike hat man versucht, den Duft der Rosenblüten einzufangen, um ihn den Menschen nutzbar zu machen. Mit Ölen und Fetten ausgezogen, ergaben ihre Blütenblätter parfümierte Salben. Die Isolierung des reinen ätherischen Öles gelang jedoch erst nach der Erfindung der Wasserdampfdestillation durch die Araber. Heute ist eine Sorte der Damaszenerrose (Rosa× damascena Miller 'Trigintipetala') die wichtigste Ölrose. Um 1700 brachten die Türken die Ölrosenkultur zum Bal-

rosiers cultivés est structuré en trois niveaux : le genre, l'espèce et la variété (cultivar). Les noms de genre et d'espèce sont latinisants, la dénomination variétale est généralement un nom moderne, placé entre guillemets ('... ').

LE PARFUM DES ROSES

Dès l'Antiquité, on a cherché le moyen de capter la senteur des roses à des fins utilitaires. Leurs pétales mélangés à des corps gras et des huiles donnaient des pommades parfumées. Mais ce n'est qu'avec l'invention de la distillation et de l'alambic par les Arabes qu'on put extraire l'essence de rose. Aujourd'hui, deux espèces sont cultivées pour cet usage : le rosier de Damas (*Rosa× damascena* Miller ' Trigintipetala '), le plus important, et le rosier centfeuille (*Rosa centifolia* L.). Autour de 1700, les Turcs introduisirent la culture des rosiers dans les Balkans, laquelle ne se répandit vraiment qu'en Bulgarie, au nord de la Thrace, dans la fameuse

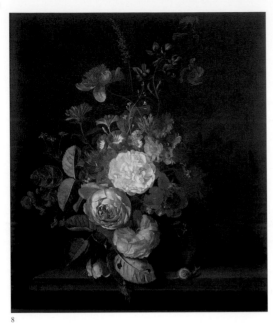

8

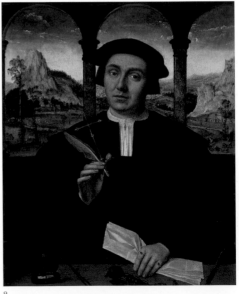

8 | JAN VAN HUYSUM (1682–1749)
Still life with flowers
Blumenstilleben
Nature morte avec fleurs
Leipzig, Museum der Bildenden Künste

9 | QUENTIN MASSYS (1465/66–1530)
Portrait of a Notary, c. 1510
Porträt eines Notars, um 1510
Portrait d'un notaire, vers 1510
Edinburgh, National Gallery of Scotland

9

has a similar composition to Bulgarian rose oil, but does have a different scent. In the perfume town of Grasse in southern France, on the other hand, a hybrid of the Provence and the French rose is used. Since the 13th century, rose water has also been used in the kitchen to flavour sauces, soups and stews. Marzipan and other confectionery are still made using rose water today. It is also used as an additive to some herb-flavoured liqueurs.

ROSES IN ART

Because of its beauty, scent and ephemerality, the rose is usually connected with three spheres of life: love, death and Elysium. According to mythology, the rose grew out of the blood of the dying Adonis. It became a symbol of Aphrodite, and the Romans also attributed it to their goddess of love. Although the rose was extolled as "the queen of flowers" even in early Greek poetry, for example in Sappho's songs of Nature, the pictorial art of the rose seems to have met with less interest. It was not until after the nat-

---

kan. Nur in Bulgarien, im Norden Thraziens, im »Tal der Rosen«, breitete sich eine Ölrosenkultur aus. Die Produktion des »Bulgarischen Rosenöls« im anatolischen Hochland der Türkei überflügelt aber heute diejenige des Ursprungslandes. Dort herrschen auf einer Höhe von 1000 m besonders günstige ökologische Bedingungen für den Anbau der Damaszenerrose. Das »Bulgarische Rosenöl« findet in der Pharmazie und Medizin, aber auch in der Parfümerie und Kosmetik Verwendung. In Südfrankreich und Marokko wird durch Wasserdampf-destillation aus der Zentifolie ein ätherisches Öl mit ähnlicher Zusammensetzung wie das »Bulgarische Rosenöl« hergestellt, es unterscheidet sich aber im Geruch. In der Parfümstadt Grasse in Südfrankreich wird dagegen eine Hybride aus der Zentifolie und der Essigrose verwendet. Seit dem 13. Jahrhundert spielt Rosenwasser auch in der Küche eine Rolle, zum Würzen von Saucen, Suppen oder Ragouts. Marzipan und andere Konditorwaren werden noch heute mit Rosenwasser zubereitet, es dient ferner als Zusatz für manche Kräuterliköre.

« Vallée des roses ». Toutefois, l'essence de rose « bulgare » qu'on produit actuellement sur les hauts plateaux d'Anatolie surpasse celle du pays d'origine. A une altitude de 1000 m, les conditions écologiques se prêtent parfaitement bien à la culture du rosier de Damas. L'essence de rose « bulgare » a des applications diverses, tant dans le domaine pharmaceutique que thérapeutique, mais aussi dans l'industrie cosmétique et la parfumerie. Dans le midi de la France et au Maroc, on extrait de la rose centfeuille une essence qui a une composition analogue à celle de l'essence de rose « bulgare », mais dont la senteur est différente. En revanche, à Grasse, on cultive un hybride de centfeuille et de rosier gallique. L'eau de rose joue également un rôle en cuisine depuis le 13e siècle : elle a servi à aromatiser les sauces, les potages ou les ragoûts. Les confiseries et la pâte d'amandes sont encore de nos jours aromatisées à l'eau de rose. Enfin, elle est employée comme additif dans certaines liqueurs.

uralistic decoration of Minoan and Mycenian art that individual motifs, such as the rose, were remoulded into strictly stylised plant forms, such as the rosette. A clear rose bud can however be seen on coins from Rhodes. Roses came to Rome from Greece early on. From the 3rd century BC until the fall of the Roman Empire, the rose is frequently mentioned in literature and also played an important role in the cult of death. Roses can also be found depicted in mosaics, and in frescoes in catacombs, especially in early Christian art. As the Christian church spread across Europe, the rose, which had previously been a symbol of Venus, came to symbolise the martyrs and Christ's Passion. In Roman times, however, roses were portrayed so generally, that it is impossible to identify them with any degree of certainty. In the Middle Ages, the rose becomes the embodiment of love and of spiritual and earthly beauty. It also became the preferred symbol of the Virgin Mary, the white rose representing her humility, the red her love. The red rose is also a symbol of the martyrs.

ROSEN IN DER KUNST

Aufgrund von Schönheit, Duft und Vergänglichkeit steht die Rose allgemein in Beziehung zu Liebe, Tod und Paradies. Dem Mythos nach aus dem Blute des sterbenden Adonis erwachsen, wurde sie zum Sinnbild der Aphrodite; auch bei den Römern ist sie der Liebesgöttin zugeordnet. Obwohl die Rose schon in der frühen griechischen Dichtung wie zum Beispiel den Naturliedern Sapphos als »Königin der Blumen« besungen wird, scheint die darstellende Kunst ihr weniger Interesse entgegengebracht zu haben. Dem naturalistischen Ornament in der minoischen und mykenischen Kunst folgt die Umprägung von individuellen Motiven wie der Rose zu streng stilisierten Pflanzenformen, beispielsweise der Rosette. Eine deutliche Rosenknospe läßt sich aber zum Beispiel auf Münzen aus Rhodos erkennen. Von Griechenland aus sind die Rosen früh nach Rom gekommen, vom 3. Jahrhundert v. Chr. bis zum Niedergang des römischen Reiches erscheinen sie in der Literatur häufig, außerdem spielen sie im Totenkult eine wichtige Rolle.

LES ROSES DANS L'ART

En raison de sa beauté, de son parfum et de sa vie brève, la rose est associée à trois grandes notions : amour, mort et paradis. Dans la mythologie grecque, la rose, née du sang d'Adonis mourant, était le symbole d'Aphrodite. Pour les Romains aussi, elle symbolisait Vénus, déesse de l'amour. Bien que les poètes grecs, comme Sappho, aient chanté la rose, « reine des fleurs », les arts plastiques semblent s'être peu intéressés à elle. L'ornement naturaliste de l'art minoen et mycénien fit place à des motifs aux formes végétales très stylisées, comme la rosette. Mais on peut distinguer encore un bouton de rose sur des pièces de monnaie de Rhodes, par exemple. Les roses sont passées très tôt de la Grèce à Rome. Du 3e siècle avant notre ère jusqu'à la chute de l'empire romain, la rose apparaît souvent dans la littérature. Par ailleurs, elle jouait un rôle important dans le culte des morts. On trouve des roses sur des mosaïques, des fresques de cata-

Artists have highlighted these various levels of significance as a central theme in various pictures: as the Madonna standing by a rose bush or rose-covered sceptre or in the rose-covered Hortus conclusus. In the 15th century, the latter gave rise to the picture type of the Madonna sitting in front of a rose trellis. This symbolism is particularly clear in the devotional pictures *Madonna in the Rose Bower* (ill. 7) by the most important painter of the Cologne School, Stefan Lochner (1405/15–1451), and *Madonna of the Rose Hedge* by Martin Schongauer (1445–1491). Schongauer's painting shows two different roses. The white, semi-double rose is thought to be *Rosa × alba* L. 'Semiplena', the red one *Rosa gallica* L. Roses cut in wood or stone above confessional boxes symbolise secrecy, hence the phrase "sub rosa". This symbolism also explains the *Portrait of a Notary* (ill. 9) by Quentin Massys (1465/66–1530).

Depictions of roses became more frequent in Italian art from about the 15th century and were painted with increasing accuracy. Today, three

In der frühchristlichen Kunst finden sich Rosen in Mosaiken und auf Fresken der Katakomben. Als die christliche Kirche sich in Europa ausbreitete, entwickelte sich die Rose zum Symbol der Märtyrer und der Passion. Zu römischer Zeit sind die Rosen dann so allgemein dargestellt worden, daß ihre Identifizierung nicht möglich ist. Im Mittelalter wird die Rose zum Inbegriff der Minne sowie der geistlichen und weltlichen Schönheit. Sie entwickelt sich damit zum bevorzugten Mariensymbol; die weiße Rose steht für ihre Sittsamkeit, die rote für ihre Liebe.

Diese Bedeutungsebenen werden von den Künstlern in verschiedenen Bildfindungen thematisiert: als stehende Madonna mit Rosenstock oder Rosenzepter sowie im rosenbewachsenen Hortus conclusus, woraus im 15. Jahrhundert der Bildtypus der vor einem Rosenspalier sitzenden Madonna erwächst. In den Andachtsbildern Muttergottes in der Rosenlaube *(Abb. 7) des bedeutendsten Malers der Kölner Schule Stefan Lochner (1405/15–1451) und Martin Schongauers (1445–1491)* Maria im Rosenhag *wird diese Symbolik beson-*

combes. Avec la propagation du christianisme en Europe, la rose, autrefois symbole de Vénus, devient celui des martyrs et de la Passion. Cependant, à l'époque romaine, les roses étaient représentées si schématiquement qu'il est difficile de les reconnaître. Au Moyen Age, la rose incarne l'amour courtois, la beauté temporelle et spirituelle. Elle prend ainsi une dimension mystique et devient le symbole de la Vierge Marie. La rose blanche représente sa vertu, la rouge, son amour.

Ces différents sens sont thématisés dans la peinture : Madone assise, un sceptre de roses ou un rosier à la main, ou figurée dans le « Hortus conclusus » couvert de roses. Ces représentations donneront naissance au 15ᵉ siècle à l'archétype de la Madone assise devant un espalier de roses. C'est dans le tableau pieux *Madone à la roseraie* (ill. 7) du plus grand peintre de l'école de Cologne, Stefan Lochner (1405/15–1451), et celui de Martin Schongauer (1445–1491), *Vierge au buisson de roses*,

roses can be recognised from the paintings: the red, single French rose, the white, double White Rose of York and its pink form. *The Birth of Venus* (ill. 6) by the Florentine painter, Sandro Botticelli (1445–1510) is worth mentioning here. The cascading roses can be identified as *Rosa* × *alba* L. The White Rose of York is depicted in other paintings by Botticelli. The only one of his paintings to show a red rose, probably a French rose, is *La Primavera*.

The Provence and damask roses are depicted in the paintings of the great Dutch and Flemish masters. Jan Bruegel the elder (1568–1625), Rachel Ruysch (1664–1750) and Jan van Huysum (1682–1749) painted many pictures with roses (ill. 8). A work by J. Bruegel the elder, *The Allegory of Scent*, even illustrates how roses were used. It depicts a garden with flowering plants and rose pickers with a laboratory complete with distilling equipment to produce rose water as a medicine. There is a picture by Rachel Ruysch, court painter in Düsseldorf, of an Austrian yellow rose

ders deutlich; Schongauers Gemälde weist zwei verschiedene Rosen auf, die weiße, halbgefüllte Rose ist als Rosa × alba L. *'Semiplena', die rote als* Rosa gallica L. *zu deuten. Als Symbol der Verschwiegenheit stehen über Beichtstühlen in Holz geschnitzte oder in Stein gehauene Rosen, woher der Ausdruck »sub rosa« rührt, diese Symbolik verdeutlicht auch das* Porträt eines Notars *(Abb. 9) von Quentin Massys (1465 / 66– 1530).*

Etwa seit dem 15. Jahrhundert wird die Rose in der italienischen Kunst häufiger dargestellt, zudem wurden die Rosen immer genauer gemalt. Man kann heute drei Rosen auf den Gemälden erkennen: die rote einfache Essigrose, die weiße gefüllte Weiße Rose und die rosa gefärbte gefüllte Weiße Rose. Als Beispiel sei hier die Geburt der Venus *(Abb. 6) von Sandro Botticelli (1445–1510) angeführt. Die herabfallenden Rosen können als* Rosa × alba L. *identifiziert werden. Nur auf seinem Werk* Primavera *läßt sich eine rote Rose erkennen, die als Essigrose gedeutet werden kann.*

que cette symbolique florale devient limpide. Deux roses apparaissent chez Schongauer : la blanche semi-double est une *Rosa* × *alba* L. ' Semiplena', la rouge doit être une *Rosa gallica* L. Des roses, sculptées dans la pierre ou le bois, symbolisent le secret, au-dessus de confessionnaux. D'ou l'expression « sub rosa », qui équivaut à « sous le sceau du secret » comme dans le tableau de Quentin Massys (1465 / 66–1530), *Portrait d'un notaire* (ill. 9).

A partir du 15ᵉ siècle, la rose prend une place plus grande dans l'art italien. On peut reconnaître trois rosiers sur les tableaux : le rosier gallique rouge aux fleurs simples, le rosier blanc aux fleurs blanches et le rosier blanc aux fleurs doubles roses. Citons pour exemple le tableau de Botticelli (1445–1510), *Naissance de Vénus* (ill. 6) où les roses qui tombent en pluie sont des *Rosa* × *alba* L. On retrouve le rosier blanc dans d'autres œuvres de Botticelli, à l'exception toutefois du *Printemps* où figure un rosier rouge que l'on peut identifier comme une *Rosa gallica* L.

(*Rosa foetida* Herrm.), one of the west Asiatic roses brought to Spain by the Moors. The striped rose (*Rosa gallica* L. 'Versicolor') can also be recognised in the works of Dutch masters, including Redouté's teacher, Gerard van Spaendonck. As we progress through history, the cult of the rose becomes more general, and with the beginning of European garden cultivation the rose increasingly becomes a decorative or ornamental plant as well as a symbol of earthly love.

Auf den Gemälden der großen niederländischen und flämischen Meister treten sowohl die Zentifolie als auch die Damaszenerrose auf. So schufen etwa Jan Brueghel d. Ä. (1568–1625), Rachel Ruysch und Jan van Huysum zahlreiche Bilder mit Rosen (Abb. 8). Brueghels Allegorie des Geruchs stellt sogar die Anwendung von Rosen dar; es zeigt einen Garten mit Blütenpflanzen und Rosenpflückerinnen sowie ein Laboratorium mit Destillationsgeräten zur Herstellung von Rosenwasser. Von Rachel Ruysch, Hofmalerin in Düsseldorf, gibt es eine Darstellung der gelbblütigen Fuchsrose (Rosa foetida Herrm.), einer von den Mauren nach Spanien gebrachten westasiatischen Rose. Auch die Gestreifte Rose (Rosa gallica L. 'Versicolor') ist auf den Werken niederländischer Meister wiederzuerkennen, darunter auch Redoutés Lehrer Gerard van Spaendonck. Im weiteren Verlauf der Geschichte nimmt der Rosenkult breitere Formen an, mit dem Beginn der europäischen Gartenkultur wird die Rose immer mehr zur Schmuck- oder Zierpflanze und zum Symbol der weltlichen Liebe.

Le rosier centfeuille et le rosier de Damas ont eux aussi une place de choix dans les œuvres des Maîtres flamands et hollandais. Brueghel l'Ancien (1568–1625), Rachel Ruysch et Jan van Huysum ont peint des roses dans de nombreuses toiles (ill. 8). Un tableau de Brueghel l'Ancien, *Allégorie de l'odeur,* illustre même l'application médicinale des roses. On y voit, un jardin avec des arbustes à fleurs et des cueilleuses de roses ainsi qu'un laboratoire équipé d'appareils de distillation. Rachel Ruysch, peintre à la cour de Düsseldorf, a représenté un rosier fétide (*Rosa foetida* Herrm.), un rosier d'Orient introduit en Espagne par les Maures. Le rosier gallique sous sa forme bicolore (*Rosa gallica* L. ' Versicolor') est le sujet de nombreux peintres de fleurs hollandais, parmi lesquels Gerard Van Spaendonck, maître de Redouté. Par la suite, avec la naissance de l'horticulture ornementale et le goût pour les jardins, le rosier devient plante décorative et la rose symbole de l'amour charnel.

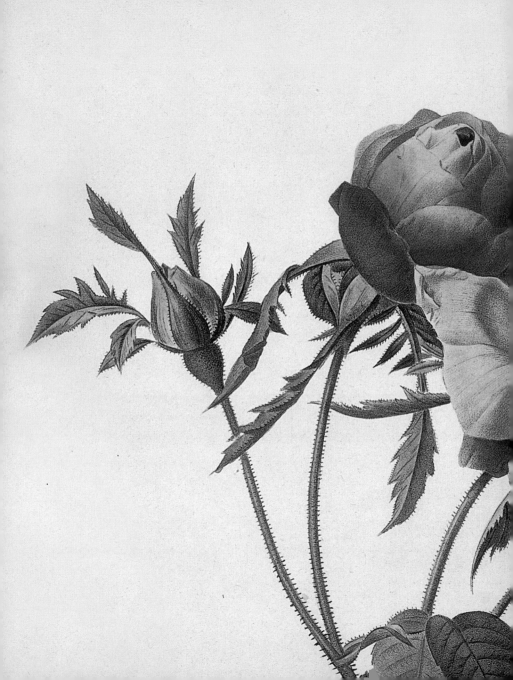

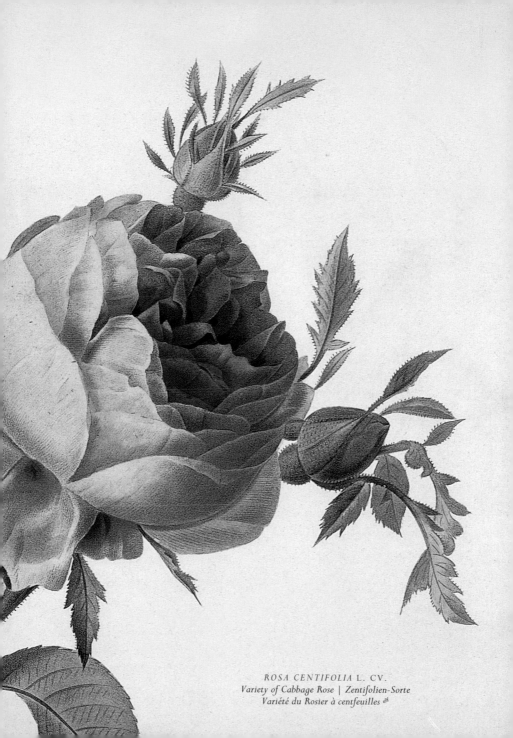

ROSA CENTIFOLIA L. CV.
Variety of Cabbage Rose | Zentifolien-Sorte
Variété du Rosier à centfeuilles

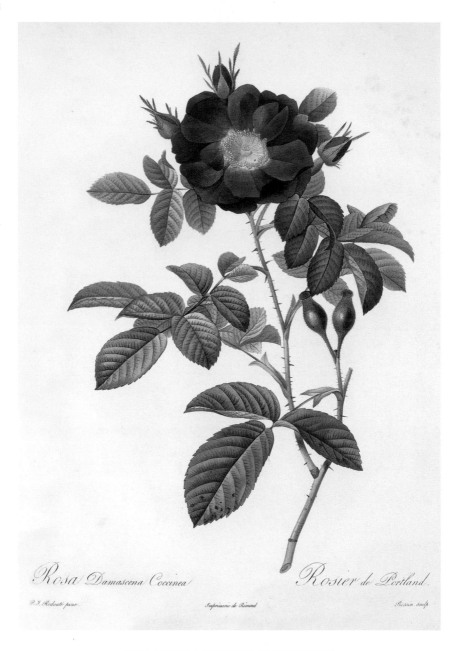

Rosa Damascena Coccinea

Rosier de Portland.

P.J. Redouté pinx.

Imprimerie de Rémond

Bessin sculp.

ROSA HYBRIDA 'DUCHESS OF PORTLAND'
Portland Rose 'Duchess of Portland' | *Portland-Rose 'Duchess of Portland'*
Rosier de Portland 'Duchess of Portland' ♔

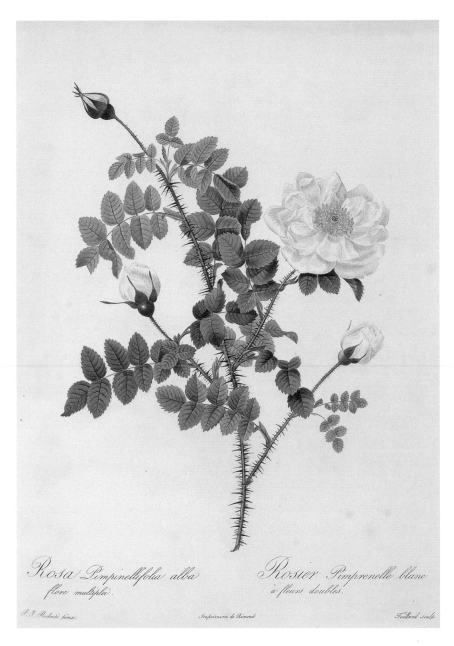

Rosa Pimpinellifolia alba
flore multiplei.

Rosier Pimprenelle blanc
à fleurs doubles.

P. J. Redouté pinx.   Imprimerie de Rémond   Teillard sculp.

ROSA PIMPINELLIFOLIA L. CV.
Semi-double variety of Burnet Rose | Halbgefüllte Bibernellrosen-Sorte
Variété du Rosier Pimprenelle à fleurs semi-doubles

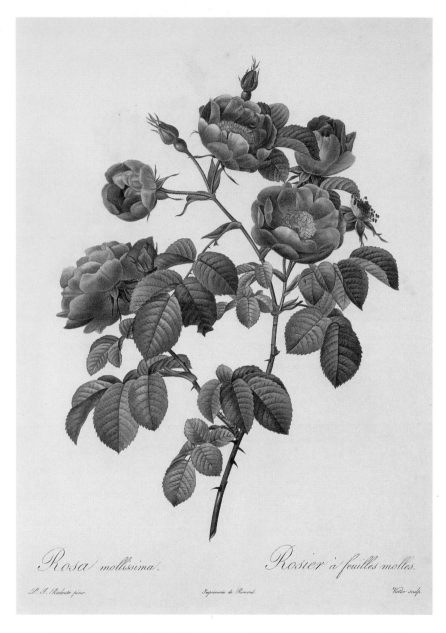

Rosa mollissima. *Rosier à feuilles molles.*

P. J. Redouté pinx. Imprimerie de Rémond. Victor sculp.

ROSA TOMENTOSA SMITH CV.
Semi-double variety of Tomentose Rose
Halbgefüllte Filzrosen-Sorte
Variété du Rosier Tomenteux à fleurs semi-doubles ⊛

ROSA MULTIFLORA THUNB. VAR.
PLATYPHYLLA REHDER ET WILSON
'SEVEN SISTERS ROSE'
Multiflora 'Seven Sisters Rose' | Vielblütige Rose 'Seven Sisters Rose' | Rosier du Japon 'Seven Sisters Rose' ⊛

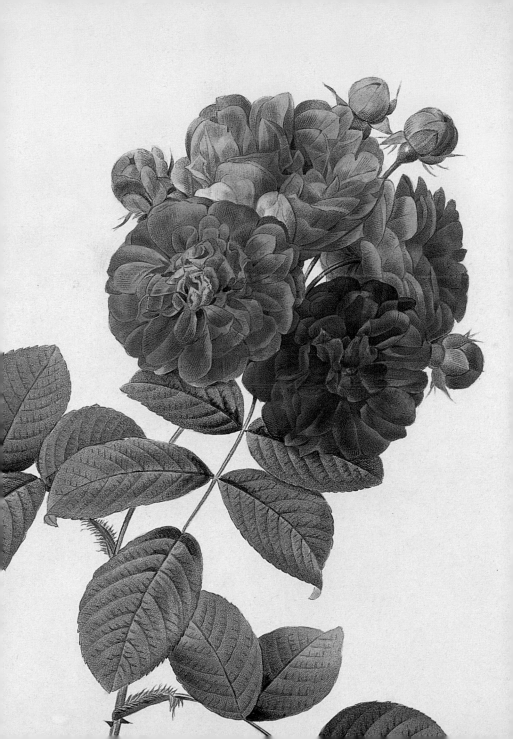

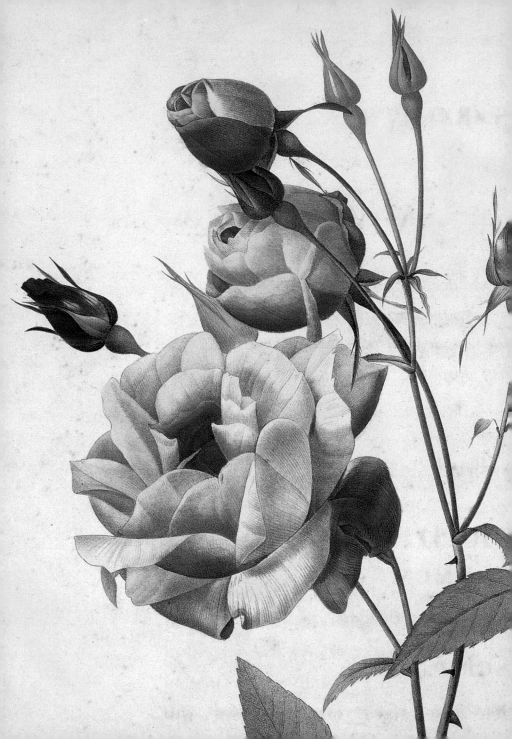

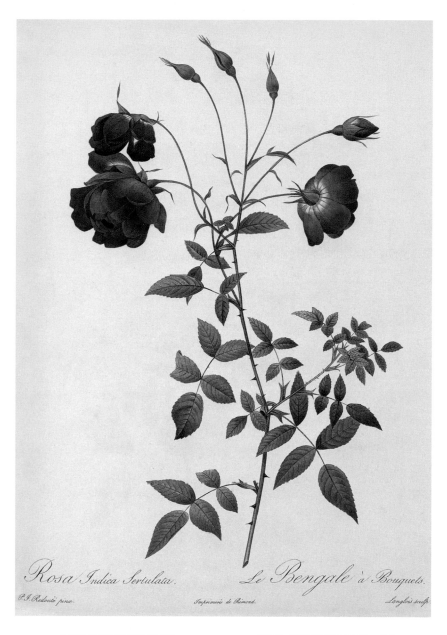

Rosa Indica Sertulata.   *Le Bengale à Bouquets.*

P.J. Redouté pinx.   Imprimerie de Remond.   Langlois sculp.

ROSA CHINENSIS JACQ.
'OLD BLUSH CHINA'
China Rose 'Old Blush China' | Chinarose 'Old
Blush China' | Rosier de Chine 'Old Blush China'

ROSA CHINENSIS JACQ. CV.
Variety of China Rose | Chinarosen-Sorte
Variété du Rosier de Chine

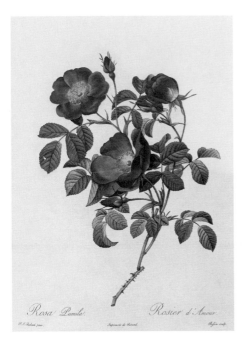

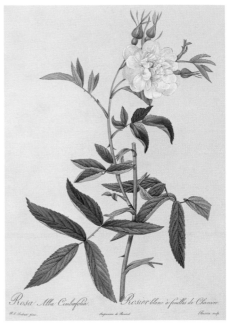

ROSA GALLICA L. VAR. PUMILA
Creeping French Rose | Kriechende Essigrose
Rosier d'Amour ❦

ROSA × ALBA L. 'À FEUILLES DE CHANVRE'
White Rose 'À feuilles de Chanvre'
Weiße Rose 'À feuilles de Chanvre'
Rosier blanc 'À feuilles de Chanvre' ❦

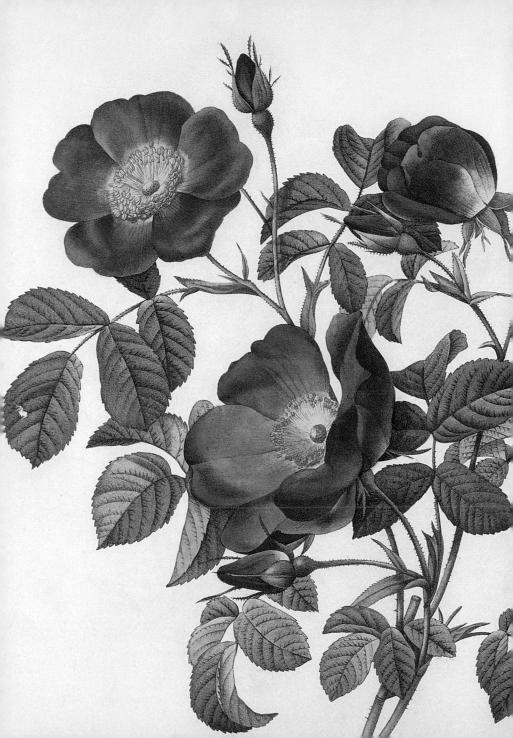

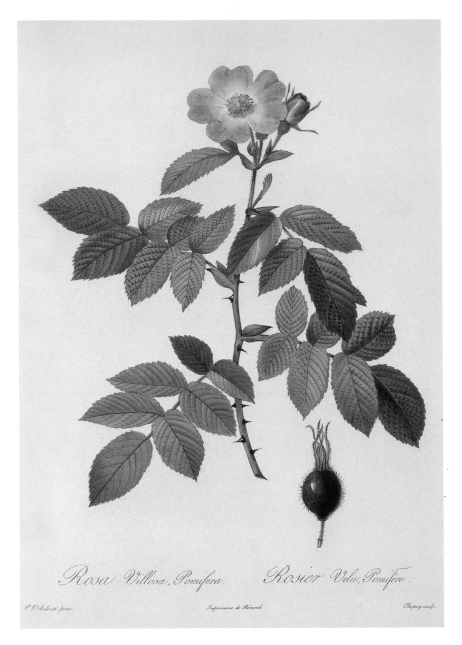

Rosa Villosa, Pomifera.   *Rosier Velu, Pomifere.*

P. J. Redouté pinx.   Imprimerie de Rémond.   Chapuy sculp.

ROSA VILLOSA L.
Apple Rose | Apfelrose | Rosier pomme

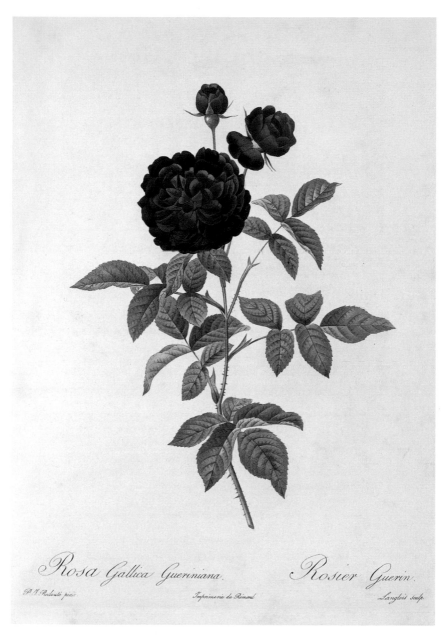

Rosa Gallica Gueriniana.   *Rosier Guerin.*

P. J. Redouté pinx.   Imprimerie de Rémond   Langlois sculp.

? *ROSA GALLICA* L. × *ROSA CHINENSIS* JACQ.
French Rose hybrid | Essigrosen-Hybride | Rosier Guerin

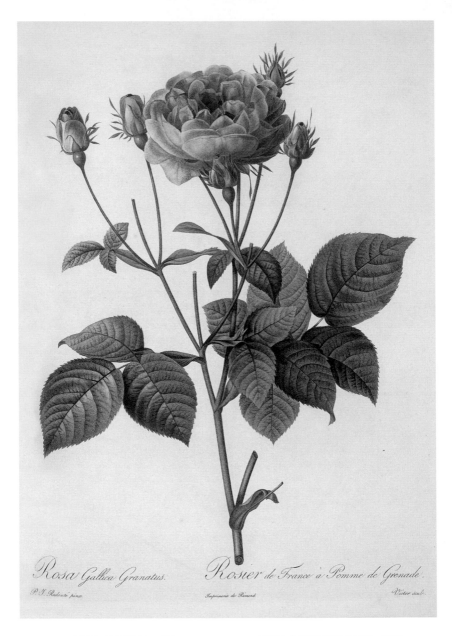

Rosa Gallica Granatus.   *Rosier de France à Pomme de Grenade.*

P. J. Redouté pinx.   Imprimerie de Rémond   Victor sculp.

ROSA GALLICA L. CV.
Variety of French Rose | *Essigrosen-Sorte*
Variété du Rosier de France ᵉᵗ

ROSA CHINENSIS JACQ. VAR.
SEMPERFLORENS KOEHNE
'SLATER'S CRIMSON CHINA'
Monthly Rose 'Slater's Crimson China' | *Monatsrose 'Slater's Crimson China'* | *Rosier mensuel 'Slater's Crimson China'* ᵖ¹ᵃ

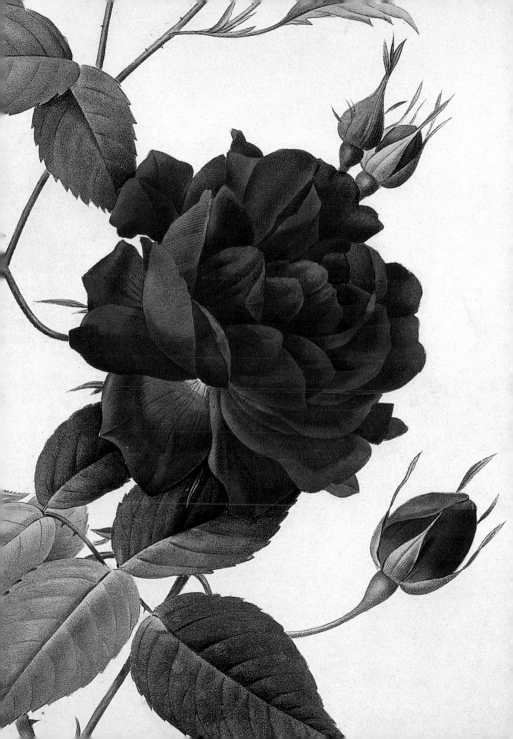

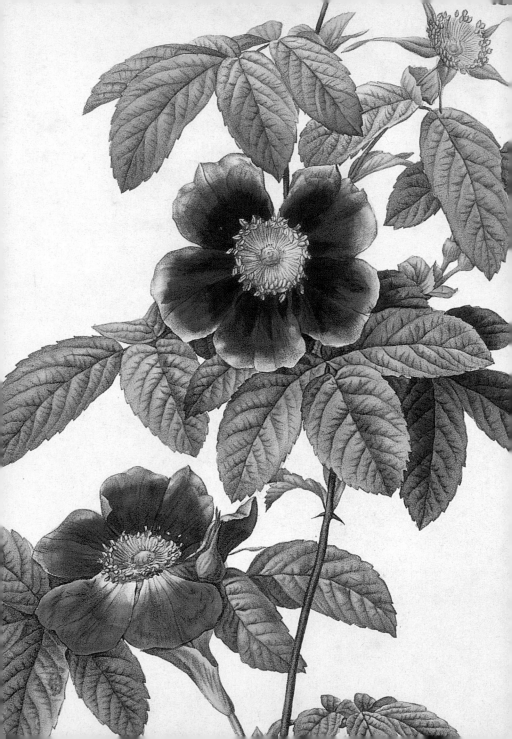

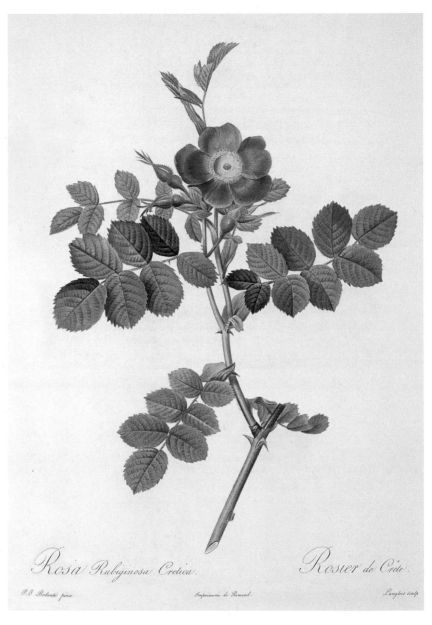

Rosa Rubiginosa Cretica.　　　　　*Rosier de Crète.*

P. J. Redouté pinx.　　　　　Imprimerie de Remond.　　　　　Langlois sculp.

ROSA MAJALIS HERRM.
May Rose | Mairose | Rosier de Mai ❧

ROSA RUBIGINOSA L.
Sweet Briar | Weinrose | Rosier rubigineux ❧

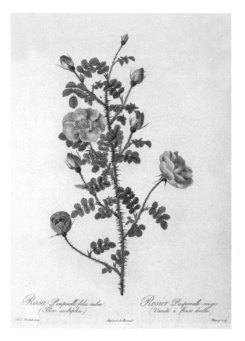

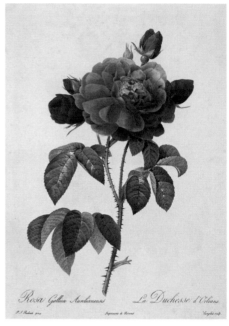

ROSA PIMPINELLIFOLIA L. 'DOUBLE PINK
SCOTCH BRIAR'
Burnet Rose 'Double Pink Scotch Briar'
Bibernellrose 'Double Pink Scotch Briar'
Rosier Pimprenelle 'Double Pink Scotch Briar'

ROSA GALLICA L. CV. ? 'DUCHESSE
D'ORLÉANS'
French Rose ? 'Duchesse d'Orleans'
Essigrose ? 'Duchesse d'Orleans'
Rosier de France ? 'Duchesse d'Orléans'

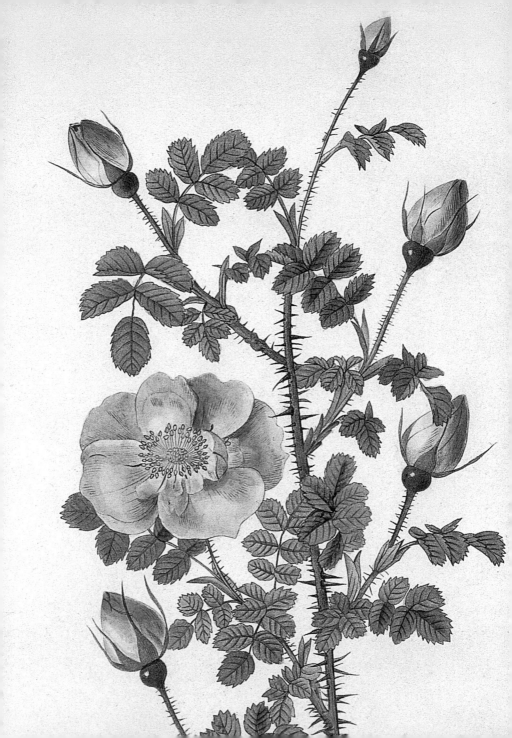

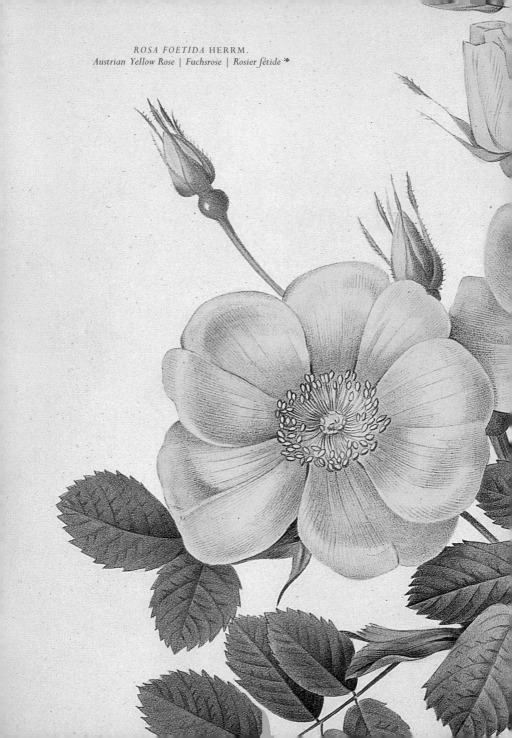

ROSA FOETIDA HERRM.
Austrian Yellow Rose | Fuchsrose | Rosier fétide ✣

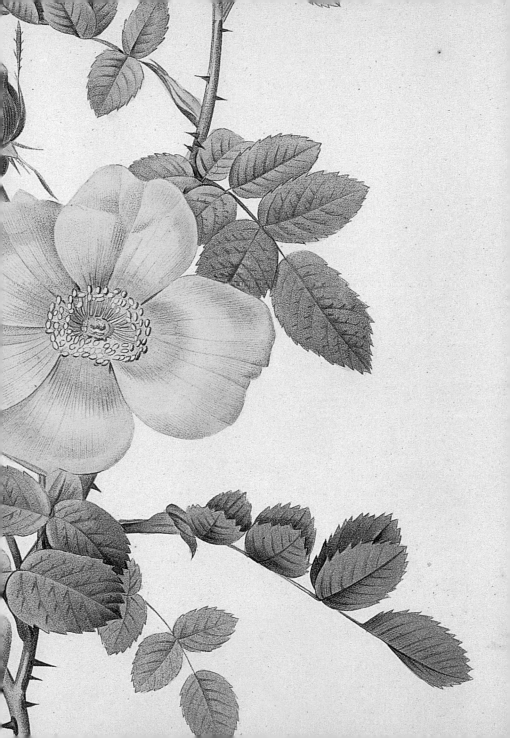

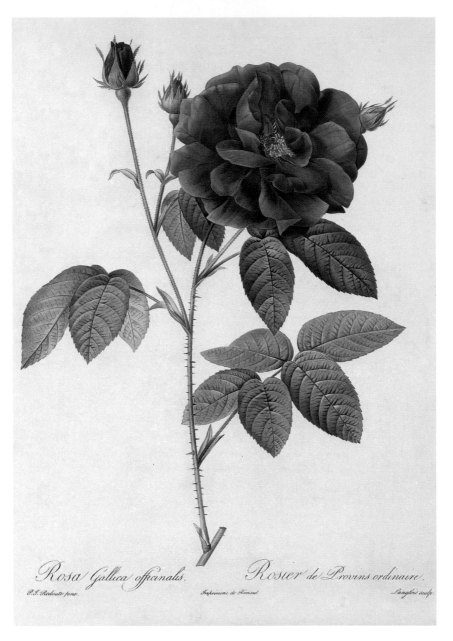

Rosa Gallica officinalis.   *Rosier de Provins ordinaire.*

P.J. Redouté pinx.   Imprimerie de Rémond   Langlois sculp.

ROSA GALLICA L. 'OFFICINALIS'
Apothecary's Rose | Apothekerrose | Rosier des Apothicaires

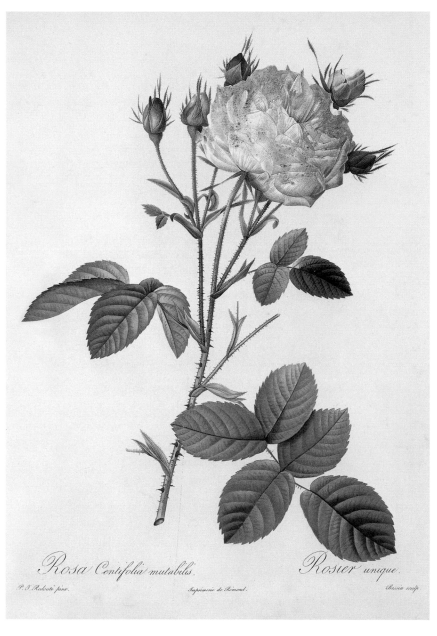

Rosa Centifolia mutabilis.   *Rosier unique.*

P. J. Redouté pinx.   Imprimerie de Rémond.   Bessin sculp.

ROSA CENTIFOLIA L. 'UNIQUE BLANCHE'

Cabbage Rose 'White Provence' | Zentifolie 'Unique blanche' | Rosier à centfeuilles 'Unique blanche'

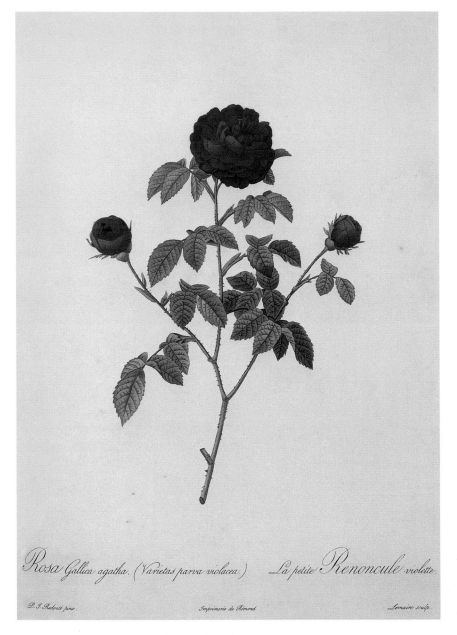

Rosa Gallica agatha. (Varietas parva violacea.)   *La petite Renoncule violette.*

P. J. Redouté pinx.   Imprimerie de Rémond   Lemaire sculp.

ROSA GALLICA L. CV. / *ROSA CENTIFOLIA* L. CV.
Variety of French Rose or Cabbage Rose | Essigrosen- oder Zentifolien-Sorte
Variété du Rosier de France ou du Rosier à centfeuilles ❧

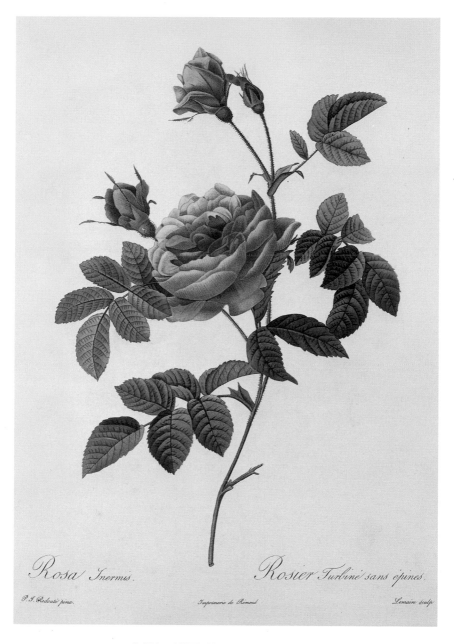

Rosa Inermis. *Rosier Turbiné sans épines.*

P. J. Redouté pinx. Imprimerie de Rémond Lemaire sculp.

ROSA × L'HERITIERANEA THORY CV.
Boursault Rose | Boursault-Rose | Rosier de Boursault ❧

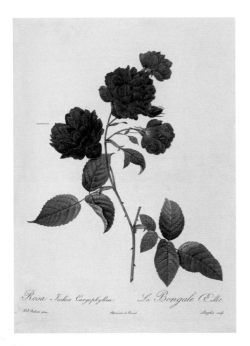

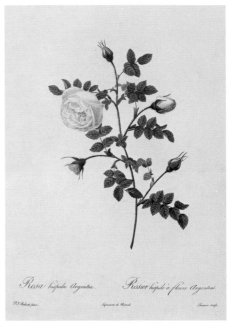

ROSA CHINENSIS JACQ. VAR.
SEMPERFLORENS KOEHNE
Monthly Rose | Monatsrose | Rosier mensuel ❧

ROSA VILLOSA L. × ROSA PIMPINELLIFOLIA L.
Apple Rose hybrid | Apfelrosen-Hybride
Rosier pomme hybride ❧

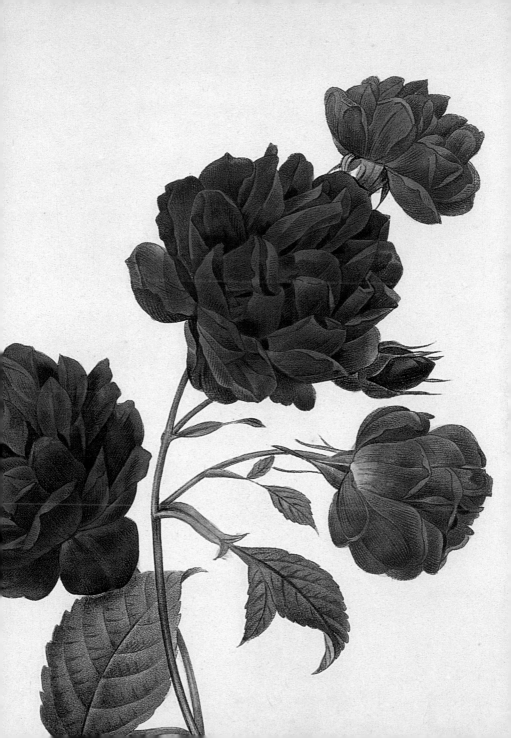

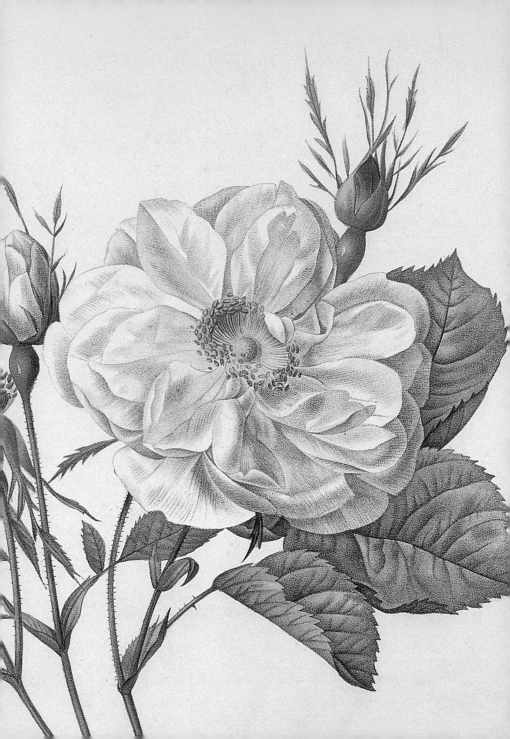

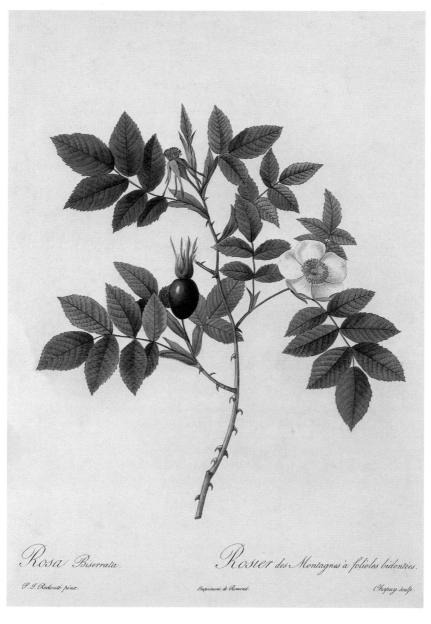

Rosa Biserrata.

Rosier des Montagnes à folioles bidentées.

P. J. Redouté pinx.

Imprimerie de Remond.

Chapuy sculp.

ROSA × ALBA L. CV.
Variety of White Rose with pinnate sepals
Weiße Rosen-Sorte mit gefiederten Sepalen
Variété du Rosier blanc

ROSA DUMALIS BECHSTEIN VAR.
MALMUNDARIENSIS FOR *BISERRATA*
? Double serrated Malmedy-Rose
? Doppeltgesägte Malmedy-Rose
? Rosier de Malmedy à folioles bidentées

54

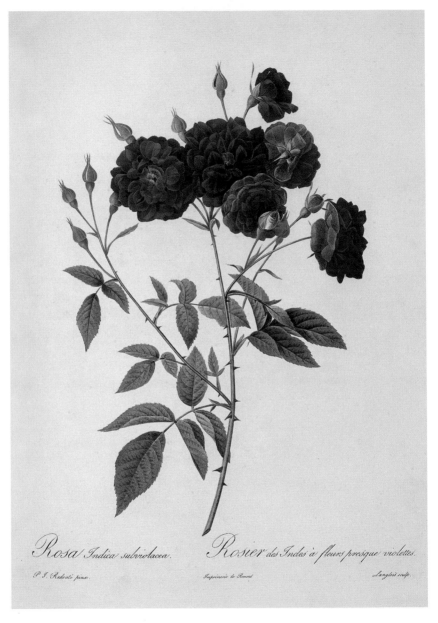

Rosa Indica subviolacea.   *Rosier des Indes à fleurs presque violettes.*

P. J. Redouté pinx.   Imprimerie de Rémond   Langlois sculp.

ROSA CHINENSIS JACQ. VAR.
SEMPERFLORENS KOEHNE
Monthly Rose | Monatsrose | Rosier mensuel ❦

ROSA GALLICA L. 'OFFICINALIS'
Apothecary's Rose | Apothekerrose
Rosier des Apothicaires ❦

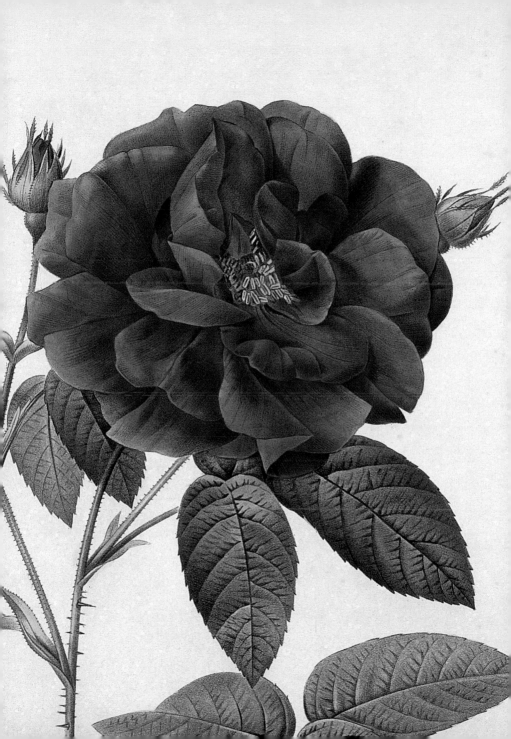

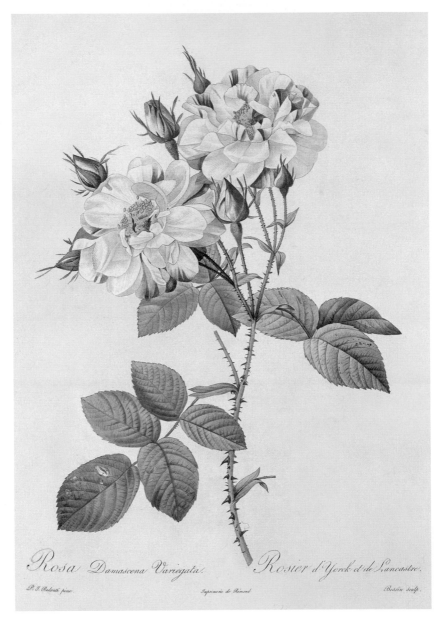

Rosa Damascena Variegata. *Rosier d'Yorck et de Lancastre.*

P. J. Redouté pinx.   Imprimerie de Rémond   Bessin sculp.

ROSA × DAMASCENA MILLER
'VERSICOLOR'
Damask Rose 'York and Lancaster'
Damaszenerrose 'York and Lancaster'
Rosier d'Yorck et de Lancastre

ROSA GALLICA L. CV. ? 'DUCHESSE
D'ORLÉANS'
French Rose ? 'Duchesse d'Orléans'
Essigrose ? 'Duchesse d'Orléans'
Rosier de France ? 'Duchesse d'Orléans'

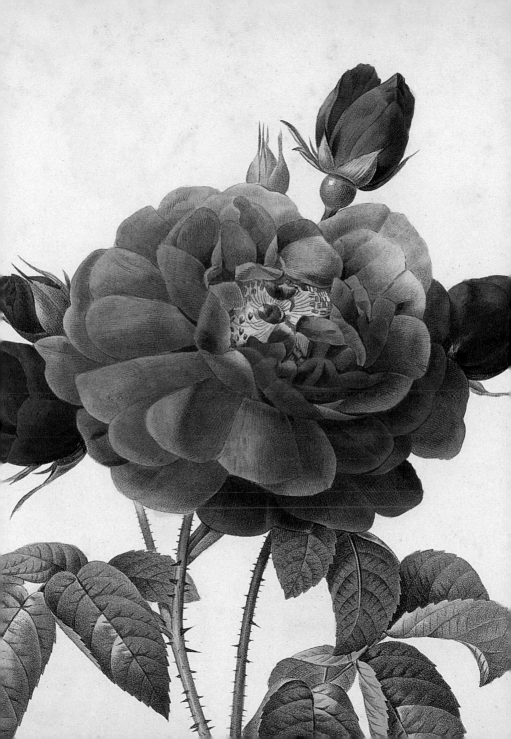

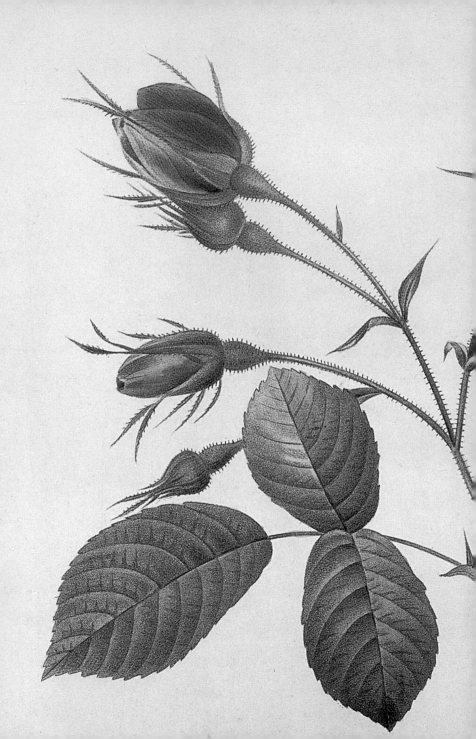

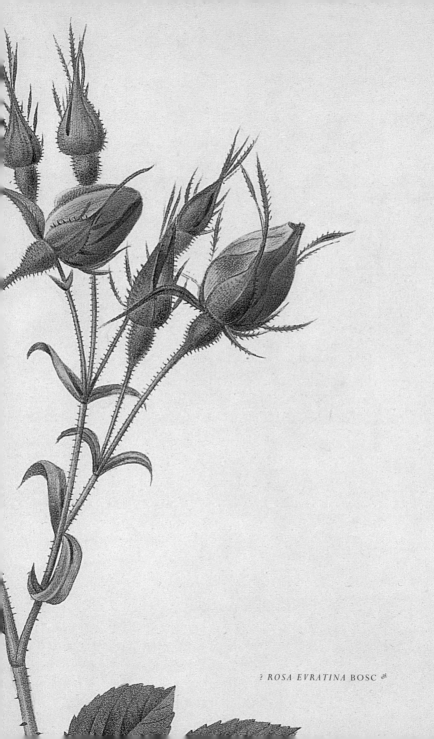

? *ROSA EVRATINA* BOSC

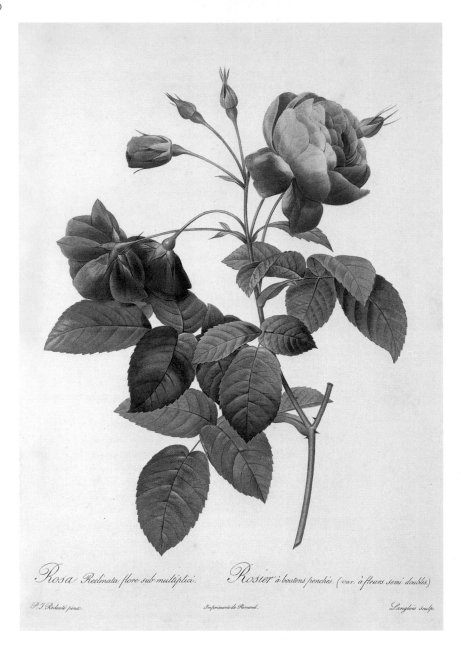

Rosa Reclinata flore sub multiplici.　　　*Rosier à boutons penchés. (var. à fleurs semi doubles.)*

P. J. Redouté pinx.　　　Imprimerie de Remond.　　　Langlois sculp.

ROSA × L'HERITIERANEA THORY
Boursault Rose | Boursault-Rose | Rosier de Boursault [bis]

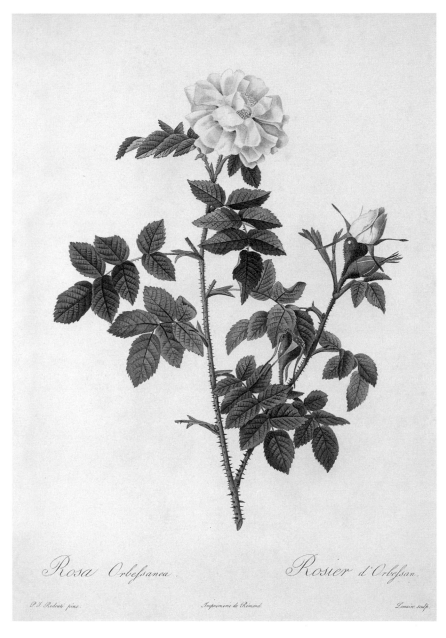

Rosa Orbeſsanea.   *Rosier* d'Orbeſsan.

P. J. Redouté pinx.   Imprimerie de Rémond.   Lemaire sculp.

ROSA × FRANCOFURTANA THORY
? 'Francofurtana' | *? Frankfurter-Rose* | *? Rosier d'Orbessan* [ssp.]

62

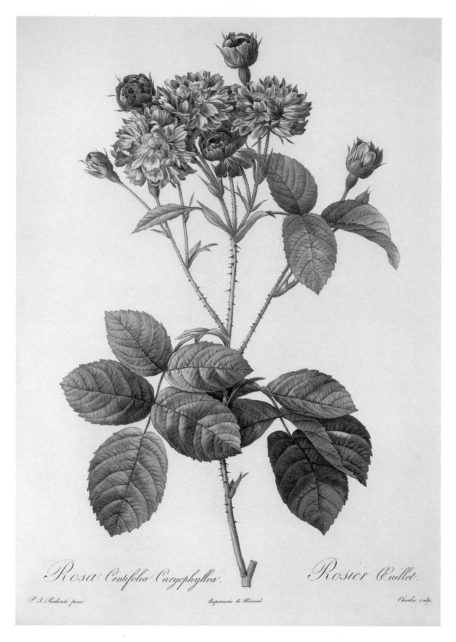

Rosa Centifolia Caryophyllea.   *Rosier Œillet.*

P. J. Redouté pinx.   Imprimerie de Rémond.   Chapin sculp.

ROSA CENTIFOLIA L. CV.
Carnation petalled variety of Cabbage Rose | Nelkenblütige Zentifolien-Sorte | Rosier œillet

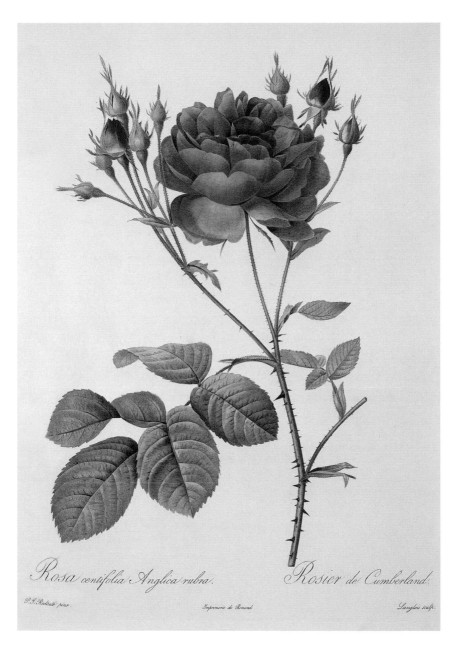

Rosa centifolia Anglica rubra.   Rosier de Cumberland.

P. J. Redouté pinx.   Imprimerie de Remond.   Langlois sculp.

ROSA CENTIFOLIA L. CV.
Variety of Cabbage Rose | Zentifolien-Sorte | Variété du Rosier à centfeuilles [et.]

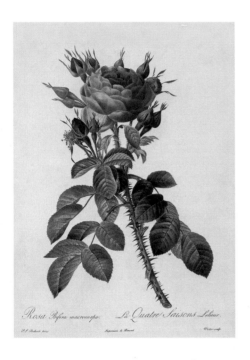

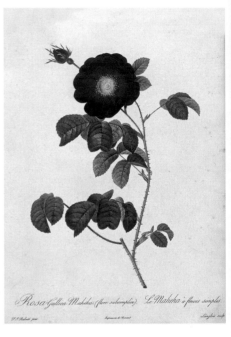

Rosa Bifera macrocarpa.   *La Quatre Saisons Lelieur.*

Rosa Gallica Mahéka (flore subsimplici).   *Le Mahéka à fleurs simples.*

ROSA × DAMASCENA MILLER × ROSA
CHINENSIS JACQ. VAR. SEMPERFLORENS
KOEHNE 'ROSE DU ROI'
Portland Rose 'Rose du Roi' | Portlandrose 'Rose du Roi'
Rosier de Portland 'Rose du Roi' ❦

ROSA GALLICA L. 'VIOLACEA'
French Rose 'Violacea' | Essigrose 'Violacea'
Rosier de France 'Violacea' ❦

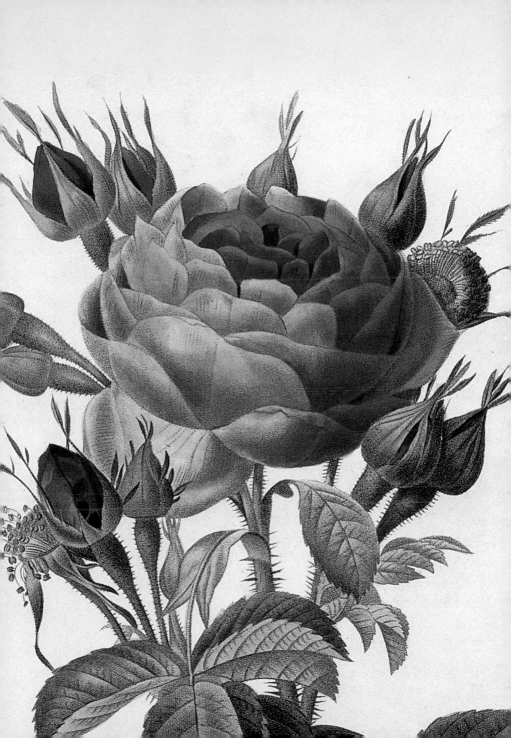

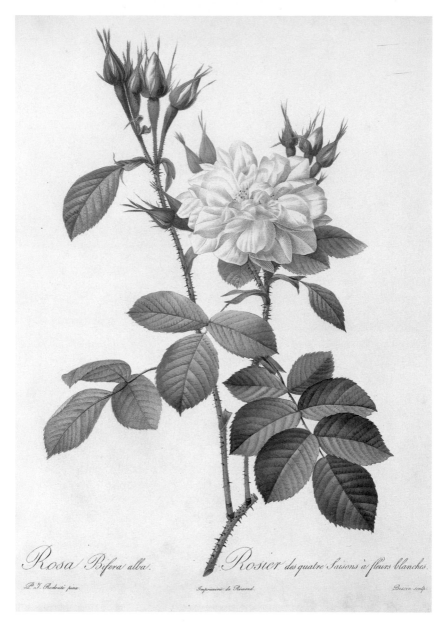

Rosa Bifera alba. *Rosier des quatre Saisons à fleurs blanches.*

P.J. Redouté pinx. Imprimerie de Rémond. Bessin sculp.

ROSA × BIFERA PERS.
White variety of Autumn Damask Rose
Weiße Herbst-Damaszenerrose
Variété du Rosier damascène d'Automne à fleurs
blanches

ROSA × DAMASCENA MILLER 'CELSIANA'
Damask Rose 'Celsiana' | Damaszenerrose 'Celsiana'
Rosier damascène 'Celsiana'

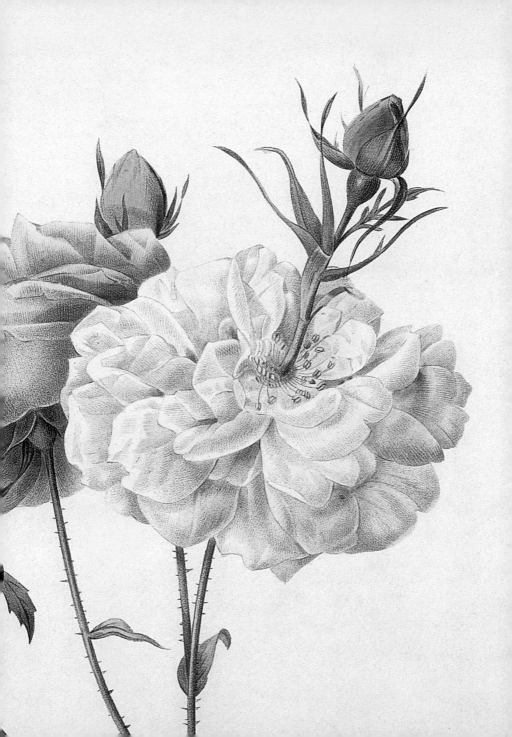

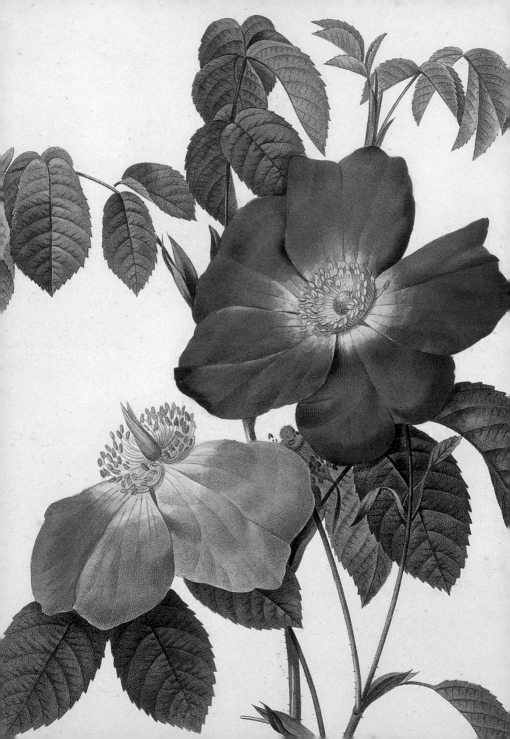

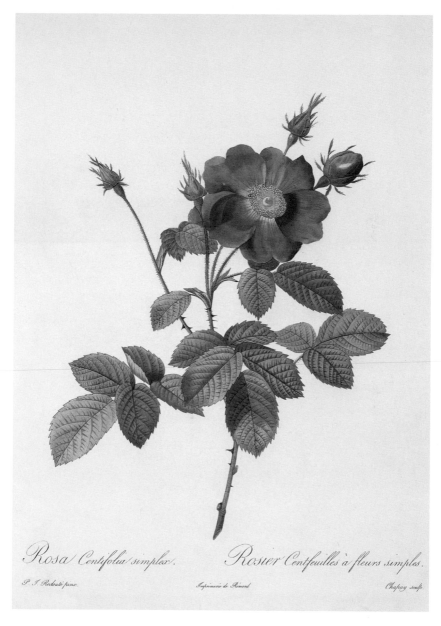

Rosa Centifolia simplex.　　*Rosier Centfeuilles à fleurs simples.*

P. J. Redouté pinx.　　Imprimerie de Rémond　　Chapuy sculp.

ROSA GALLICA L.
French Rose | Essigrose | Rosier de France

ROSA CENTIFOLIA L. 'SIMPLEX'
Single Cabbage Rose | Einfache Zentifolie
Rosier à centfeuilles à fleurs simples

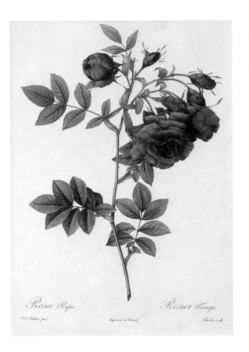

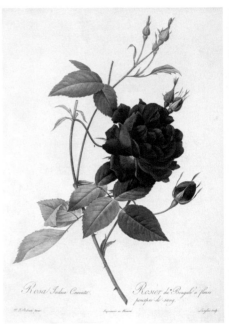

? *ROSA* × *RAPA* BOSC
? '*Rose d'Amour*' | ? '*Rose d'Amour*'
? *Rosier d'Amour* [1/2]

ROSA CHINENSIS JACQ. VAR.
SEMPERFLORENS KOEHNE
'SLATER'S CRIMSON CHINA'
Monthly Rose '*Slater's Crimson China*' | Monatsrose '*Slater's Crimson China*' | Rosier mensuel '*Slater's Crimson China*' [1/2]

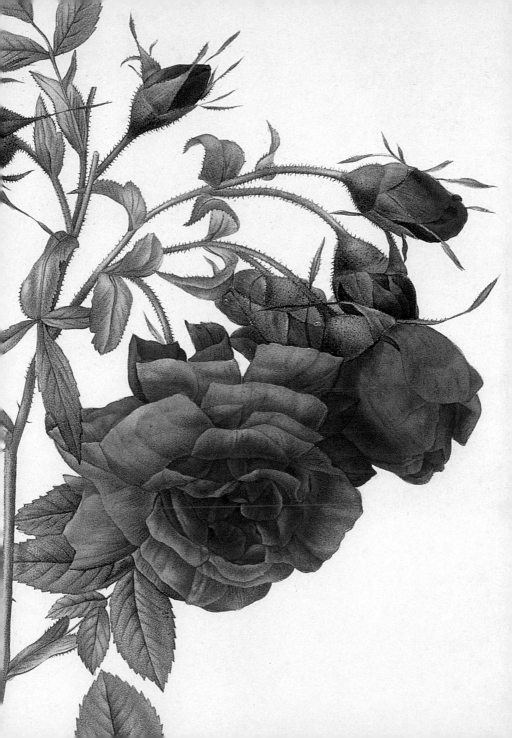

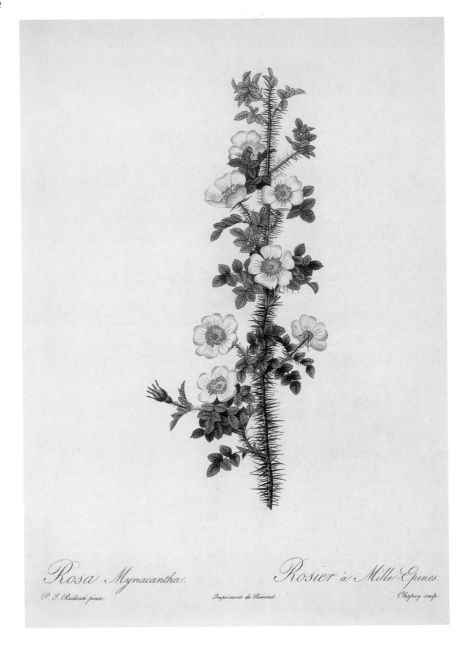

Rosa Myriacantha.   *Rosier à Mille-Épines.*

P. J. Redouté pinx.   Imprimerie de Rémond.   Chapuy sculp.

? *ROSA PIMPINELLIFOLIA* L. VAR. *MYRIACANTHA* SER.
Prickly variety of Burnet Rose | Stachelige Bibernellrosen-Sorte
Variété du Rosier Pimprenelle à mille épines ❧

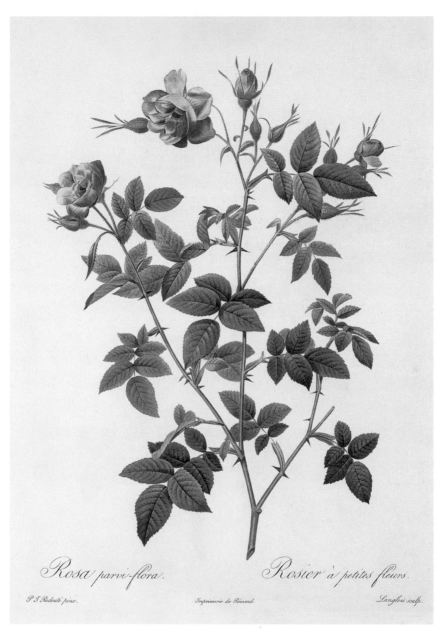

Rosa parvi-flora.   *Rosier à petites fleurs.*

P. J. Redouté pinx.   Imprimerie de Rémond.   Langlois sculp.

ROSA CAROLINA L. 'PLENA'
Double Pasture Rose | Gefüllte Wiesenrosen-Sorte | Rosier des prés à fleurs doubles [73]

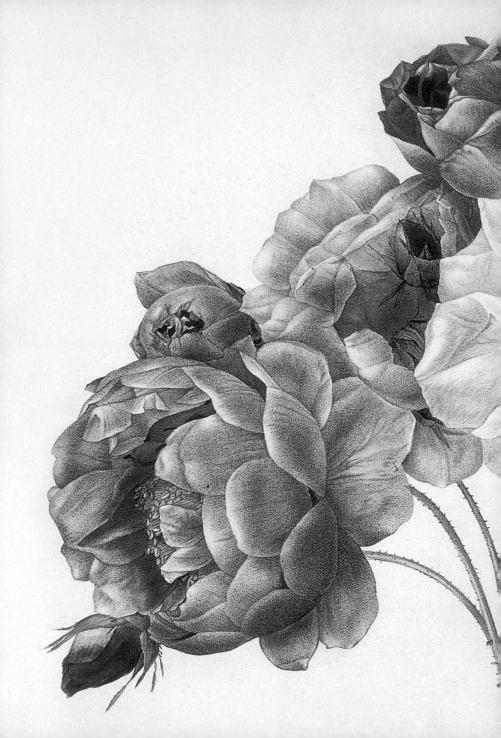

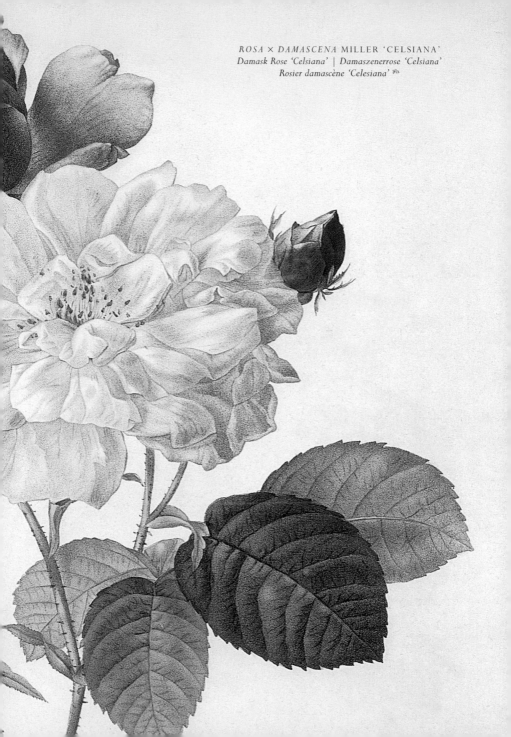

ROSA × *DAMASCENA* MILLER 'CELSIANA'
Damask Rose 'Celsiana' | Damaszenerrose 'Celsiana'
Rosier damascène 'Celesiana'

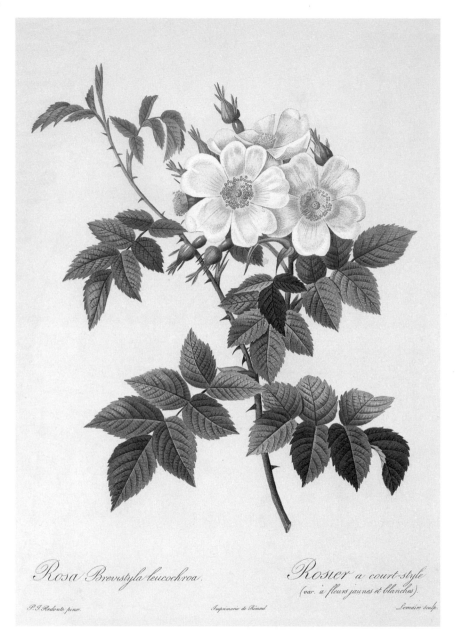

Rosa Brevistyla leucochroa.

Rosier a court-style
(var. à fleurs jaunes et blanches).

P.J.Redouté pinx.   Imprimerie de Rémond   Lemaire sculp.

ROSA STYLOSA DESV. VAR. SYSTYLA
— | Griffelrosen-Sorte | Rosier à court-style (var. à fleurs jaunes et blanches) [fr.]

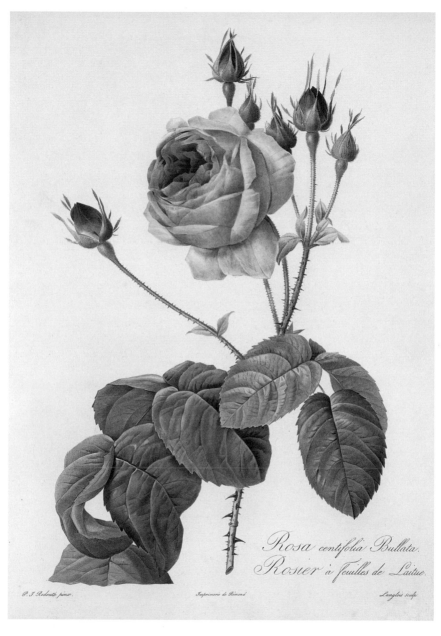

Rosa centifolia Bullata.
Rosier à feuilles de Laitue.

P. J. Redouté pinx.   Imprimerie de Rémond   Langlois sculp.

ROSA CENTIFOLIA L. 'BULLATA'
Lettuce-leaved Cabbage Rose | Salatrose | Rosier à feuilles de Laitue

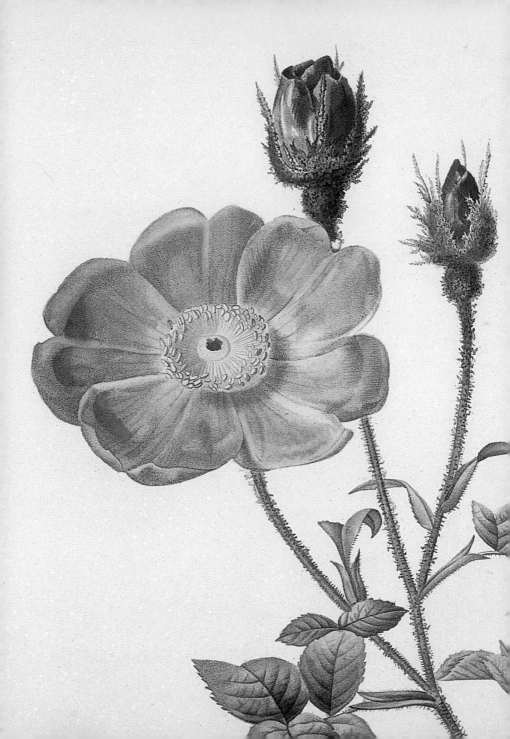

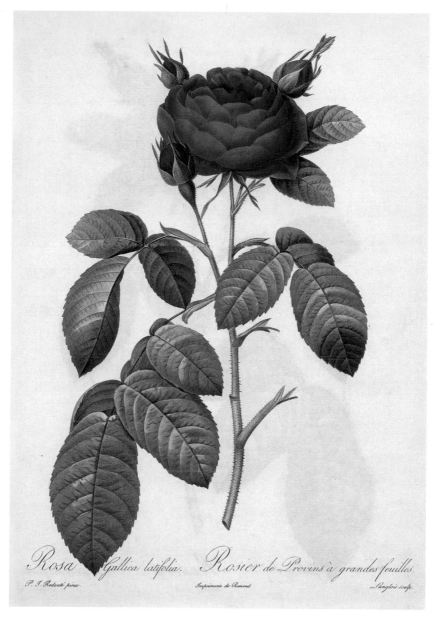

Rosa Gallica latifolia. *Rosier de Provins à grandes feuilles.*

P. J. Redouté pinx.   Imprimerie de Remond   Langlois sculp.

ROSA CENTIFOLIA L. 'ANDREWSII'
Single Moss Rose 'Andrewsii'
Einfache Moosrose 'Andrewsii'
Rosier Mousseux à fleurs simples 'Andrewsii'

ROSA GALLICA L. × ? *ROSA CENTIFOLIA* L.
Large-leaved variety of French Rose
Großblättrige Essigrosen-Sorte
Variété du Rosier de France à grandes feuilles

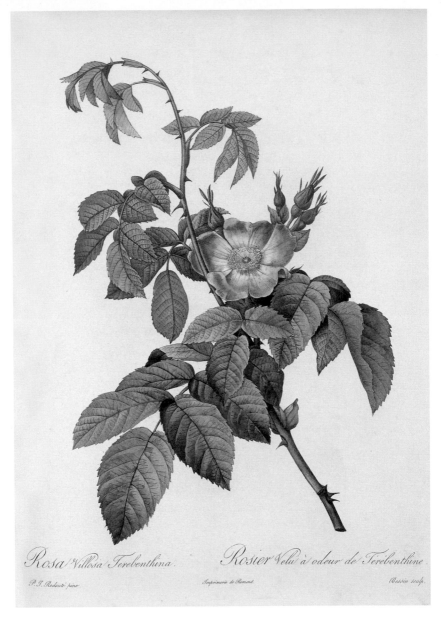

Rosa Villosa Terebenthina. *Rosier Velu à odeur de Terebenthine.*

P. J. Redouté pinx.   Imprimerie de Remond.   Bessin sculp.

ROSA L. HORT

ROSA GALLICA L. HYBR.
Provins royal | Essigrosen-Hybride
Rosier de France var. Grandeur Royale

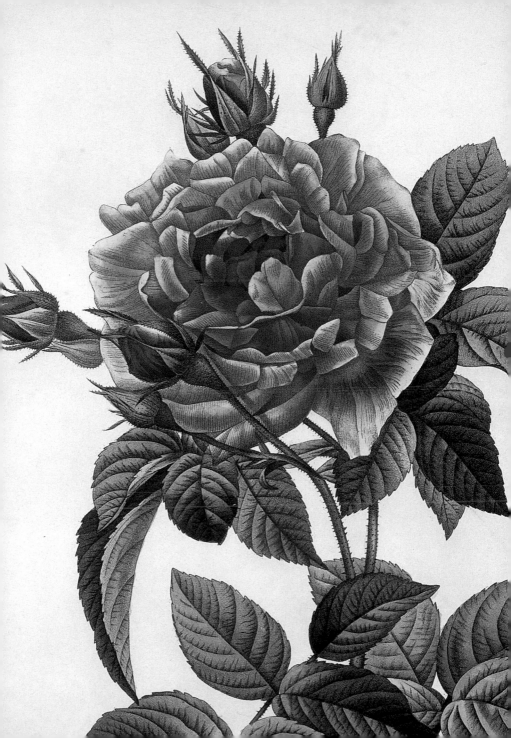

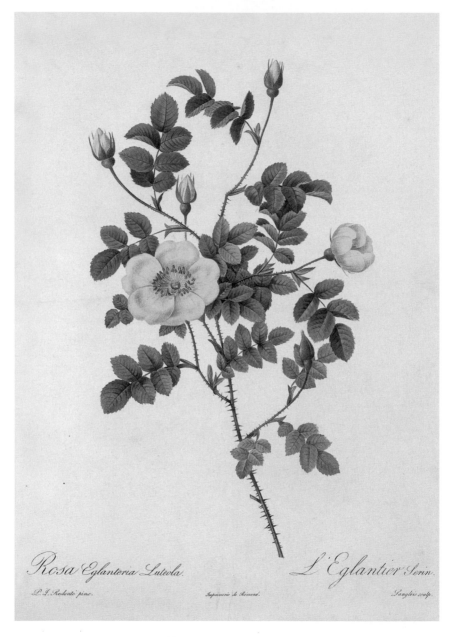

Rosa Eglanteria Luteola.

L'Eglantier Serin.

P. J. Redouté pinx.

Imprimerie de Remond.

Langlois sculp.

ROSA × HARISONII RIVERS 'LUTEA'
'Yellow Rose of Texas' | 'Yellow Rose of Texas' | Eglantier Serin

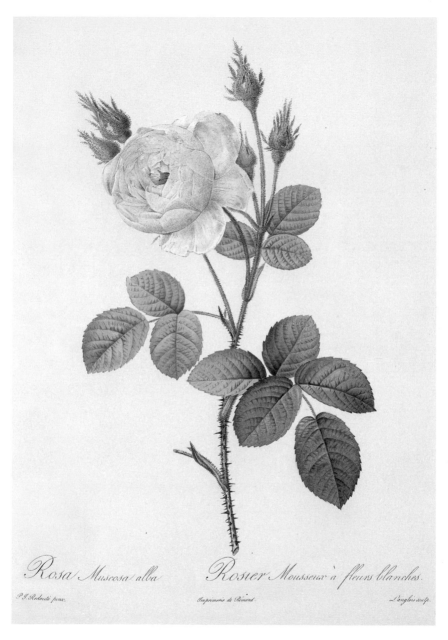

Rosa Muscosa alba

Rosier Mousseux à fleurs blanches.

P. J. Redouté pinx.   *Imprimerie de Rémond.*   *Langlois sculp.*

ROSA CENTIFOLIA L. VAR. *MUSCOSA* 'ALBA'
White Moss Rose | Weiße Moosrosen-Sorte | Rosier mousseux à fleurs blanches [83]

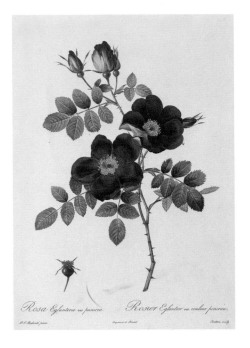

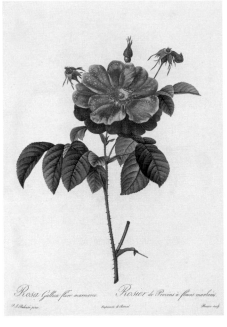

ROSA FOETIDA HERRM. 'BICOLOR'
Austrian Copper Rose | Kapuzinerrose
Rosier Capucine [bis]

ROSA GALLICA L. CV.
Marbled variety of French Rose
Marmoriert blühende Essigrosen-Sorte
Variété du Rosier de France à fleurs marbrées [cd]

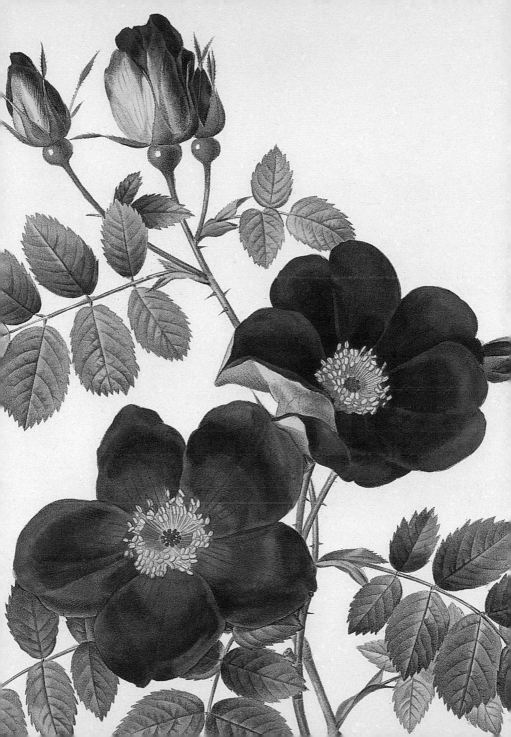

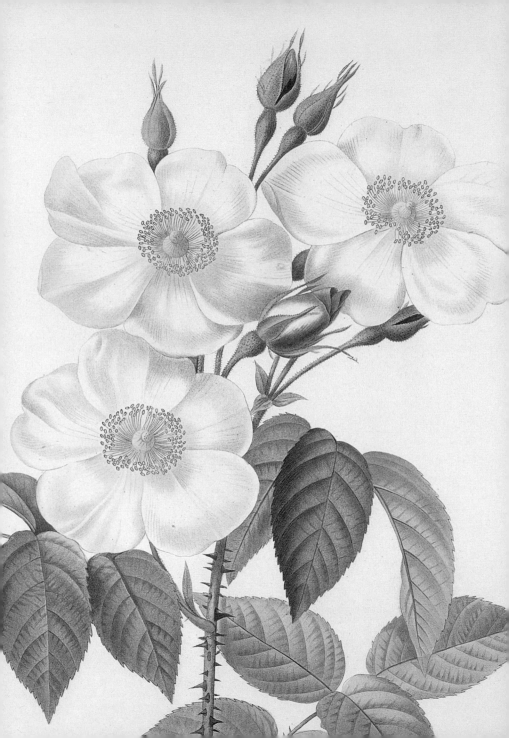

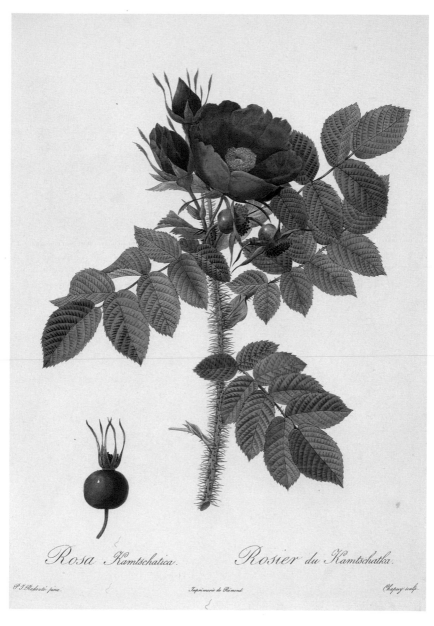

Rosa Kamtschatica.   *Rosier du Kamtschatka.*

P. J. Redouté pinx.   Imprimerie de Rémond   Chapuy sculp.

ROSA × DUPONTII DÉSÉGL.
Blush Gallica | Dupont-Rose
Rosier de Damas 'Petale teinte de rose' ❧

ROSA RUGOSA THUNB.
Japanese Rose | Kartoffelrose
Rosier à feuilles rugueuses ❧

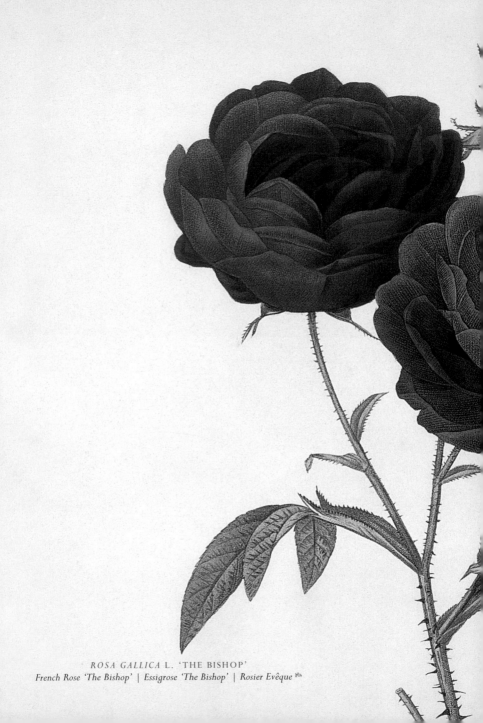

ROSA GALLICA L. 'THE BISHOP'
Frz
French Rose 'The Bishop' | Essigrose 'The Bishop' | Rosier Evêque

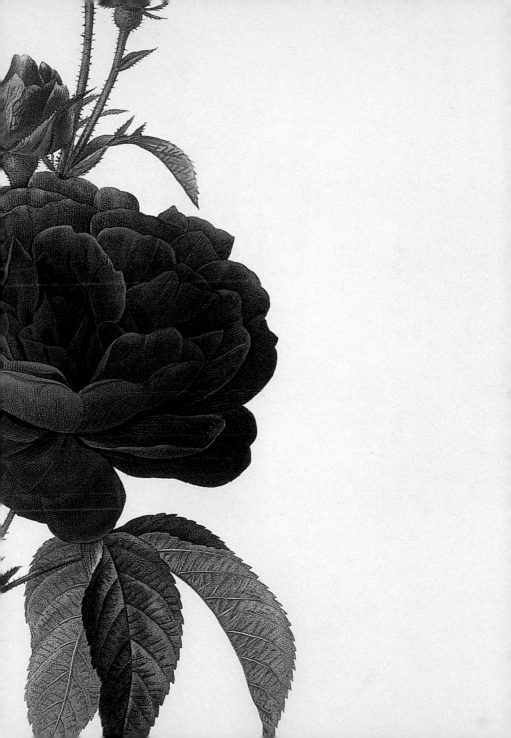

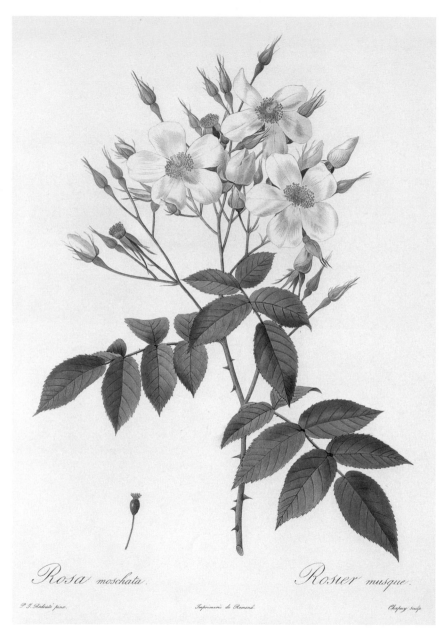

Rosa moschata.   *Rosier musque.*

P. J. Redouté pinx.   Imprimerie de Remond.   Chapuy sculp.

ROSA MOSCHATA HERRM.
Musk Rose | Moschusrose | Rosier musqué ❧

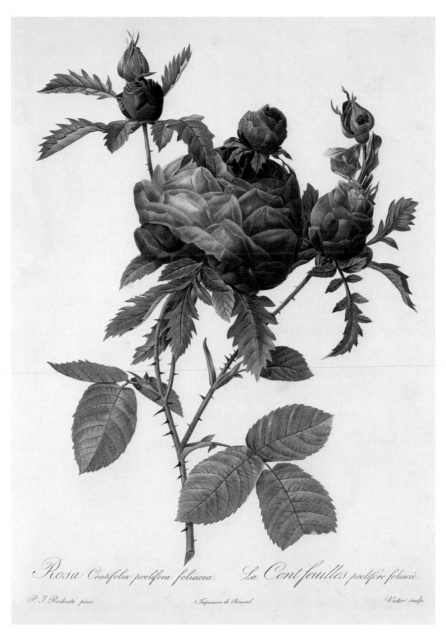

Rosa Centifolia prolifera foliacea.   *La Cent feuilles prolifère foliacée.*

P. J. Redouté pinx.   Imprimerie de Remond   Victor sculp.

ROSA CENTIFOLIA L. CV.

Variety of Cabbage Rose | Zentifolien-Sorte | Variété du Rosier à centfeuilles &

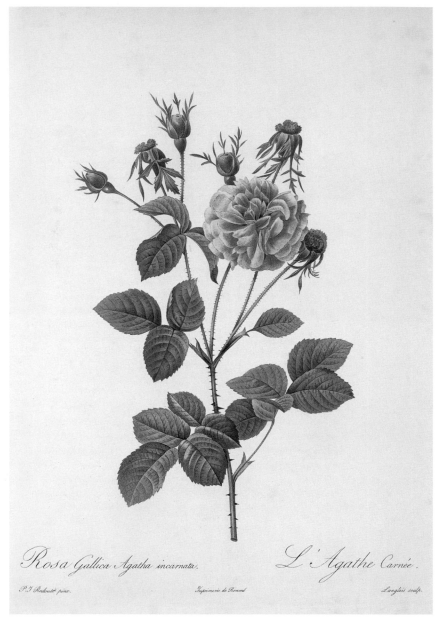

Rosa Gallica Agatha incarnata.   *L'Agathe Carnée.*

P.J. Redouté pinx.   Imprimerie de Rémond   Langlois sculp.

ROSA GALLICA L. 'AGATHA INCARNATA'
French Rose Hybrid 'Agatha Incarnata' | Essigrose 'Agatha Incarnata' | Rosier de France 'Agathe Carnée'

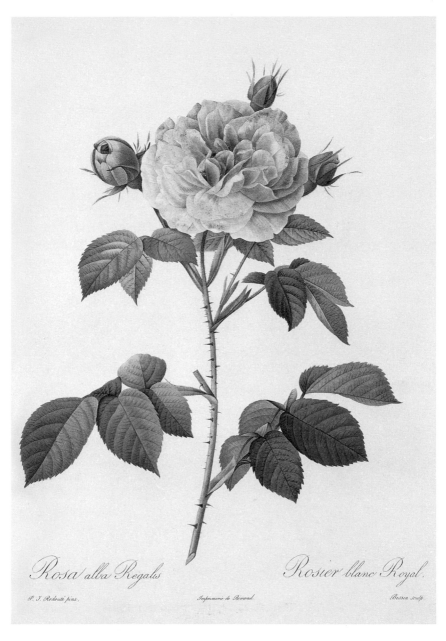

Rosa alba Regalis

Rosier blanc Royal.

P. J. Redouté pinx.　　　Imprimerie de Remond.　　　Bessin sculp.

ROSA × *ALBA* L. 'GREAT MAIDEN'S BLUSH'
White Rose 'Great Maiden's Blush' | *Weiße Rose 'Great Maiden's Blush'*
Rosier blanc 'Great Maiden's Blush' [93]

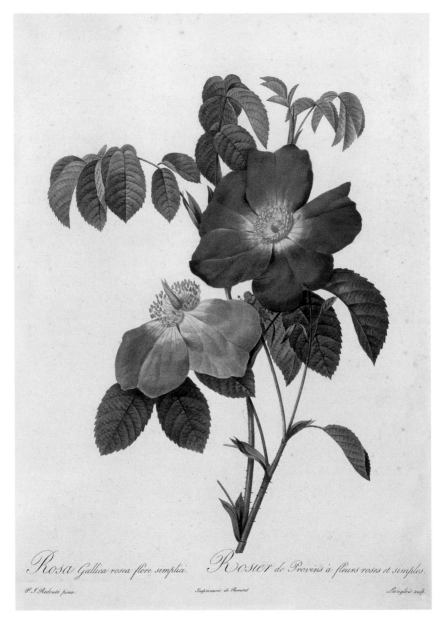

Rosa Gallica rosea flore simplici.   *Rosier de Provins à fleurs roses et simples.*

P. J. Redouté pinx.   Imprimerie de Remond   Langlois sculp.

ROSA GALLICA L.
French Rose | Essigrose | Rosier de France ⚘

ROSA CENTIFOLIA L. 'MAJOR'
Cabbage Rose | Zentifolie | Rosier à centfeuilles ⚘

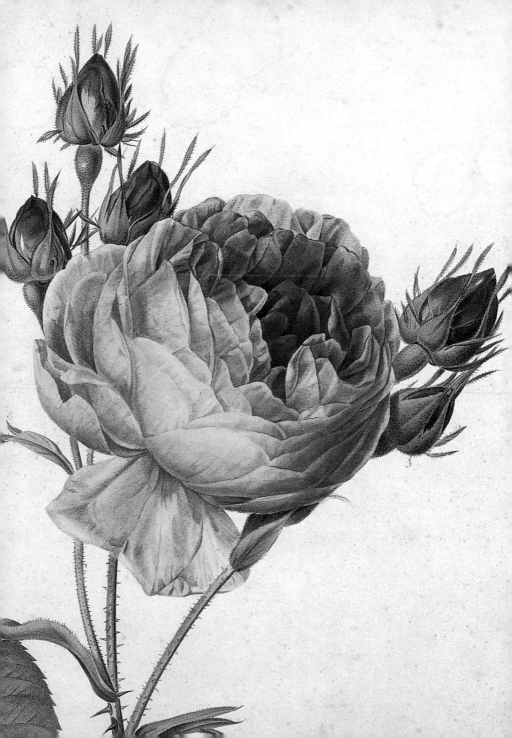

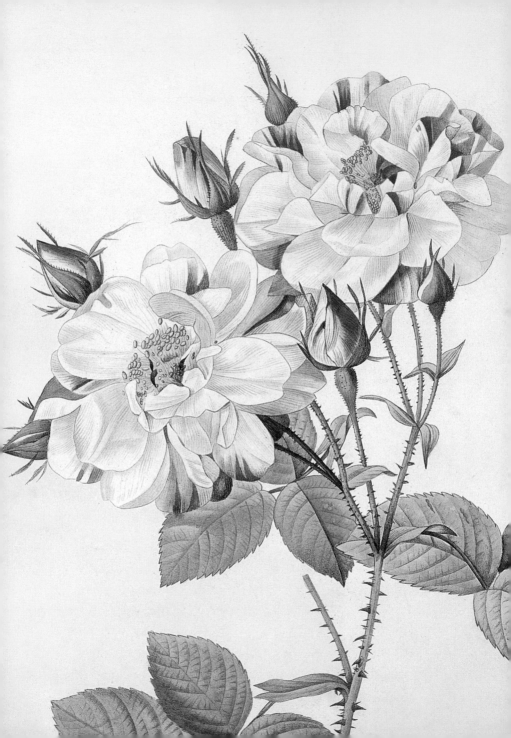

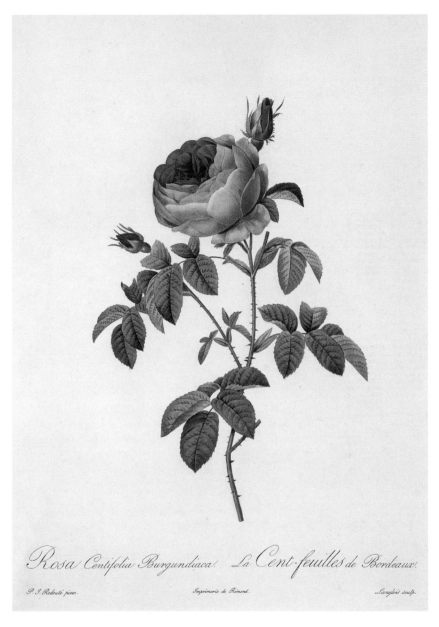

Rosa Centifolia Burgundiaca. La Cent-feuilles de Bordeaux.

P. J. Redouté pinx.   Imprimerie de Rémond.   Langlois sculp.

ROSA × DAMASCENA MILLER   *ROSA CENTIFOLIA* L.
'VERSICOLOR'   'PETITE DE HOLLANDE'
Damask Rose 'York and Lancaster'   *Cabbage Rose 'Petite de Hollande'*
Damaszenerrose 'York and Lancaster'   *Zentifolie 'Petite de Hollande'*
Rosier d'Yorck et de Lancastre ❀   *Rosier à centfeuilles 'Petite de Hollande'* ❀

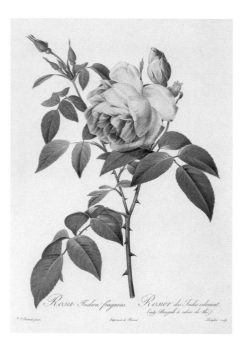

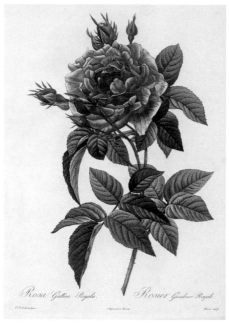

ROSA × ODORATA SWEET 'HUME'S BLUSH
TEA SCENTED CHINA'
Tea Rose 'Hume's Blush Tea scented China'
Teerose 'Hume's Blush Tea scented China'
Rosier à odeur de thé 'Hume's Blush Tea scented China' ⚘

ROSA GALLICA L. HYBR.
Provins royal | Essigrosen-Hybride
Rosier de France var. Grandeur Royale ⚘

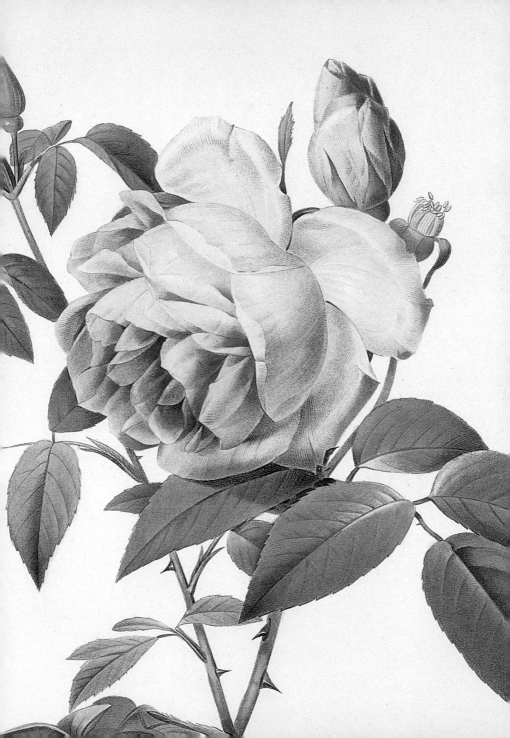

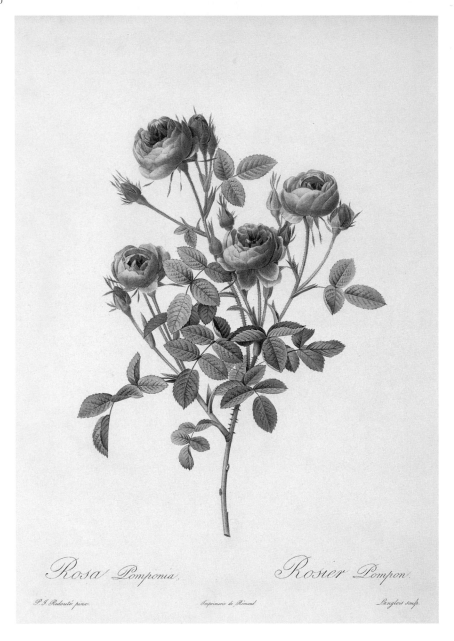

Rosa Pomponia.　　　*Rosier Pompon.*

P. J. Redouté pinx.　　Imprimerie de Rémond　　Langlois sculp.

ROSA CENTIFOLIA L. 'DE MEAUX'
Moss Rose 'De Meaux' | Dijon-Rose | Rosier Pompon 'De Meaux'

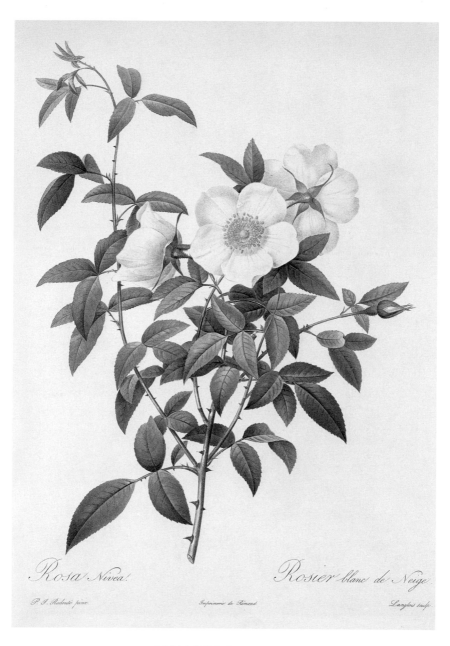

Rosa Nivea.

Rosier blanc de Neige.

P. J. Redouté pinx.

Imprimerie de Rémond

Langlois sculp.

ROSA LAEVIGATA MICHAUX
Cherokee Rose | Cherokee-Rose | Cherokee Rose ^{ya}

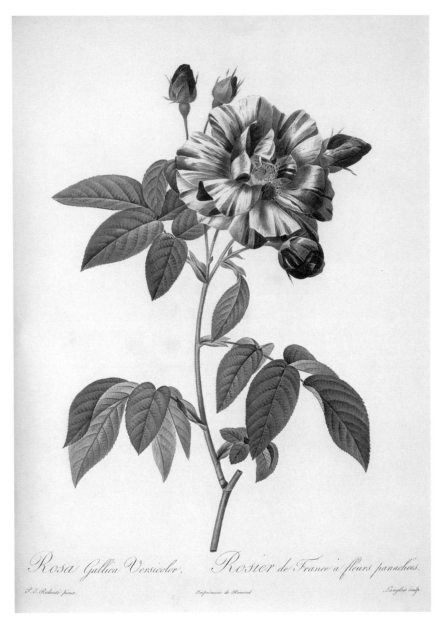

Rosa Gallica Versicolor.   *Rosier de France à fleurs panachées.*

P.J. Redouté pinx.   Imprimerie de Rémond   Langlois sculp.

ROSA GALLICA L. 'VERSICOLOR'
French Rose 'Versicolor'
Panaschiert blühende Essigrose
Rosier de France à fleurs panachées ᵖˡᵃ

ROSA CENTIFOLIA L. VAR.
MUSCOSA 'ALBA'
White Moss Rose | Weiße Moosrosen-Sorte
Rosier mousseux à fleurs blanches ᵖˡᵃ

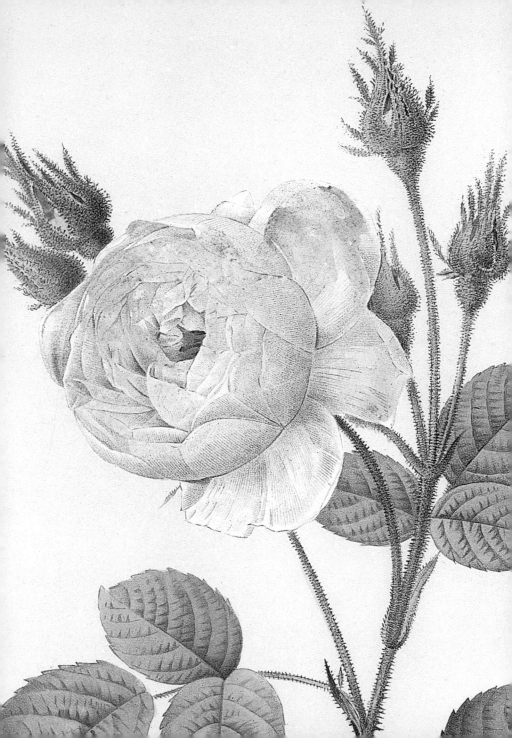

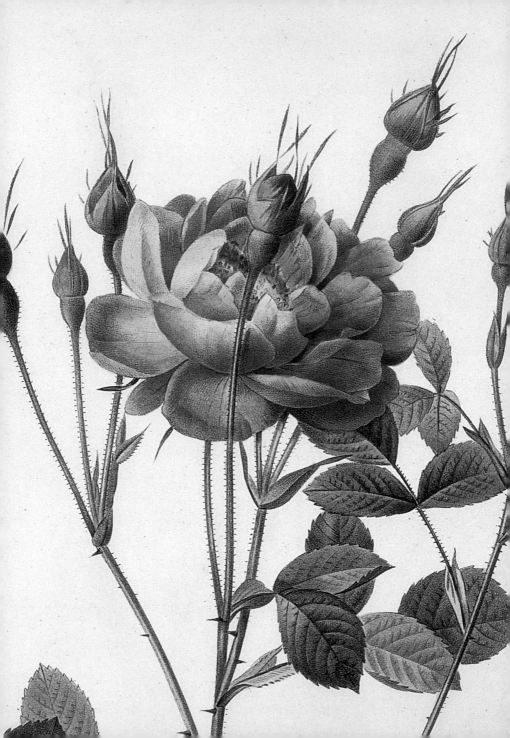

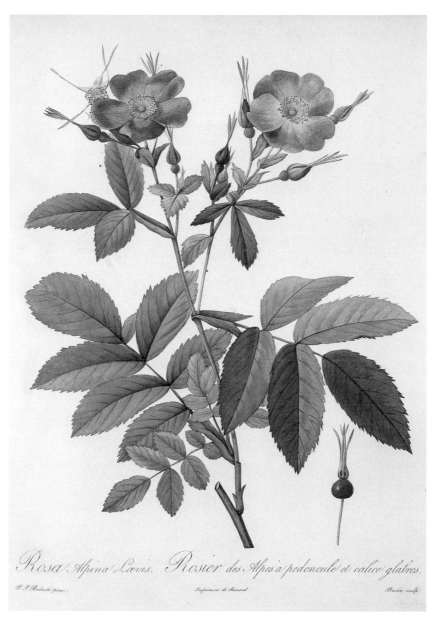

Rosa Alpina Lævis. Rosier des Alpes à pedoncule et calice glabres.

P. J. Redouté pinx.　　　Imprimerie de Remond.　　　Bessin sculp.

ROSA RUBIGINOSA L. CV.
Variety of Sweet Briar
Anemonenblütige Weinrosen-Sorte
Rosier rubigineux à fleurs d'anémone ❧

ROSA BLANDA AITON
Hudson Bay Rose | Eschenrose
Rosier à feuilles de frêne ❧

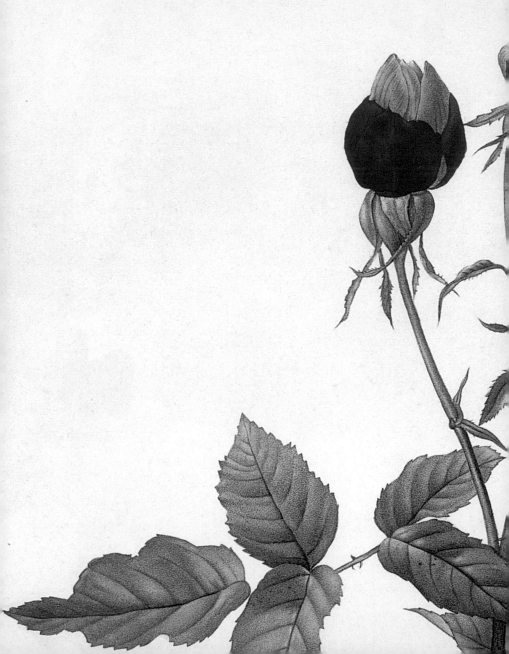

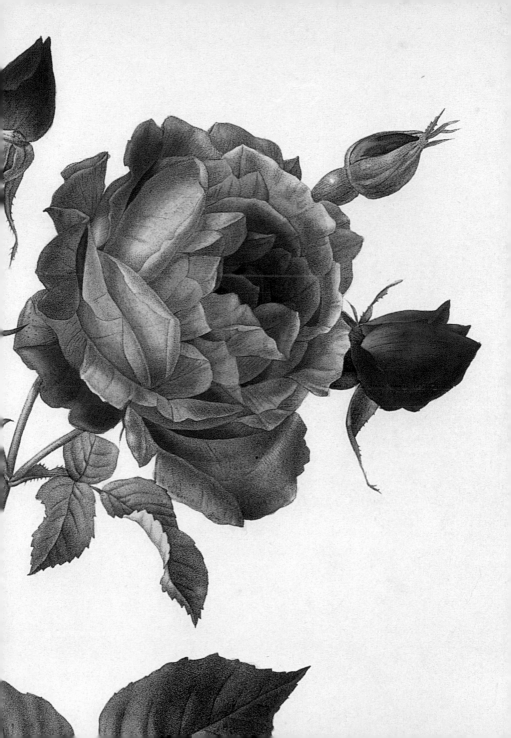

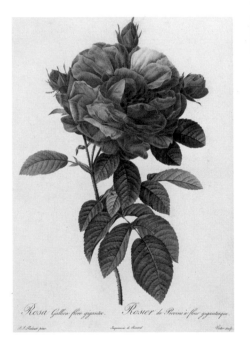 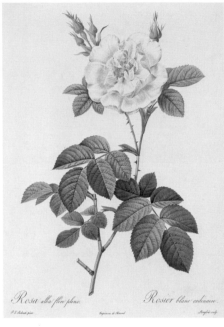

Rosa Gallica flore giganteo.   *Rosier de Provins à fleur gigantesque.*

J. J. Redouté pinx.   Imprimerie de Rémond   Victor sculp.

Rosa alba flore pleno.   *Rosier blanc ordinaire.*

P. J. Redouté pinx.   Imprimerie de Rémond   Langlois sculp.

ROSA GALLICA L. CV.
Large-flowered variety of French Rose
Großblumige Essigrosen-Sorte
Variété du Rosier de France à grandes fleurs

ROSA × *ALBA* L. 'SEMIPLENA'
Semi-double White Rose | Halbgefüllte Weiße Rose
Rosier blanc ordinaire

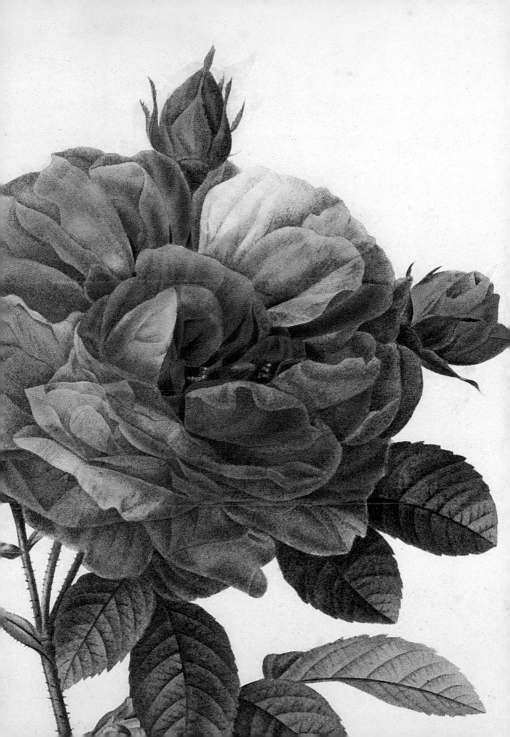

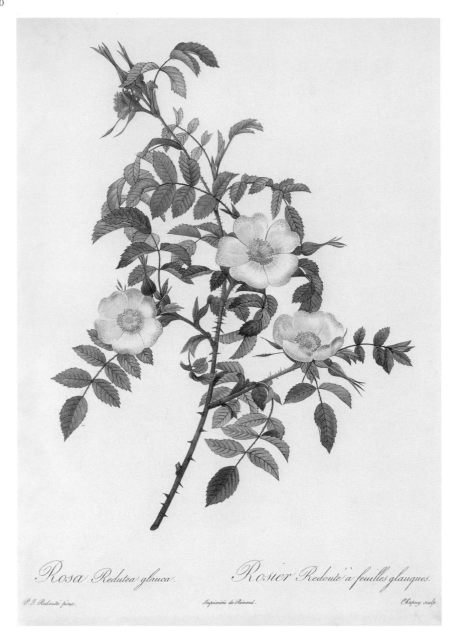

Rosa Redutea glauca.   *Rosier Redoute à feuilles glauques.*

P. J. Redouté pinx.   Imprimerie de Rémond.   Chapuy sculp.

ROSA GLAUCA POURRET × ? ROSA PIMPINELLIFOLIA L.
Redouté Rose | Redouté-Rose | Rosier Redouté 🌿

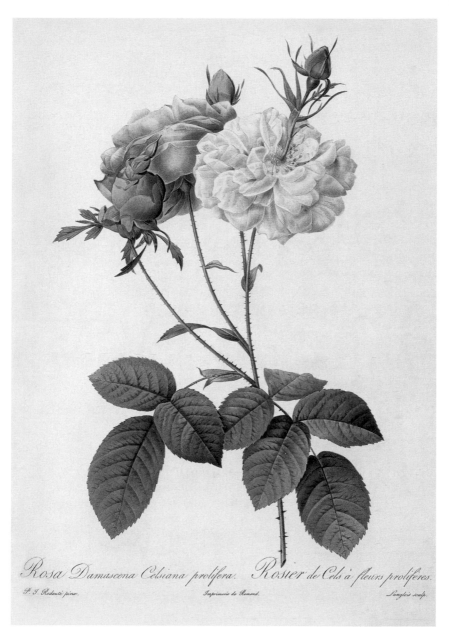

Rosa Damascena Celsiana prolifera. *Rosier de Cels à fleurs prolifères.*

P. J. Redouté pinx. Imprimerie de Remond. Langlois sculp.

ROSA × DAMASCENA MILLER 'CELSIANA'
Damask Rose 'Celsiana' | Damaszenerrose 'Celsiana' | Rosier damascène 'Celsiana' [113]

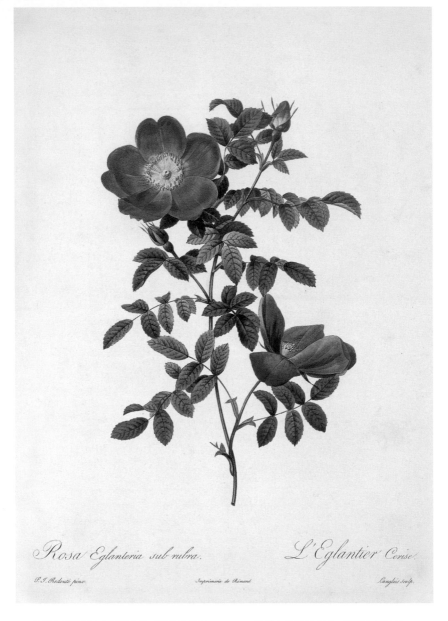

Rosa Eglanteria sub rubra.

L'Eglantier Cerise.

P.J. Redouté pinx.

Imprimerie de Rémond

Langlois sculp.

ROSA FOETIDA HERRM. 'BICOLOR'
Austrian Copper Rose | Kapuzinerrose
Rosier Capucine ᵛ⁵

ROSA GALLICA L. 'VIOLACEA'
French Rose 'Violacea' | Essigrose 'Violacea'
Rosier de France 'Violacea' ᵛ⁵

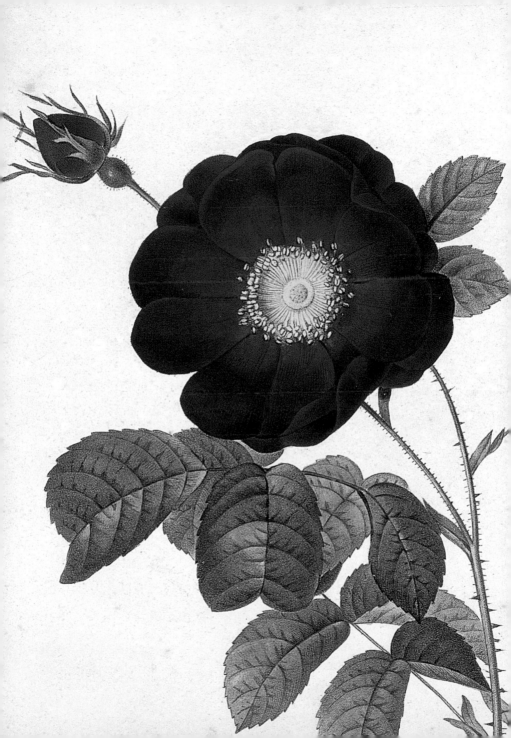

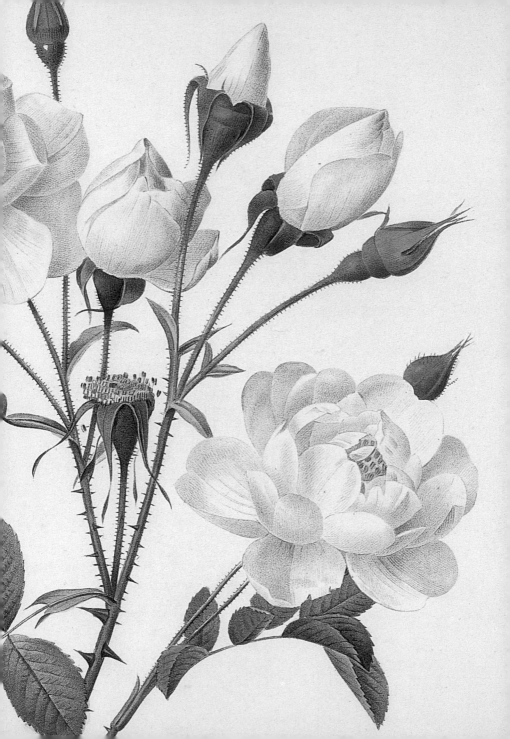

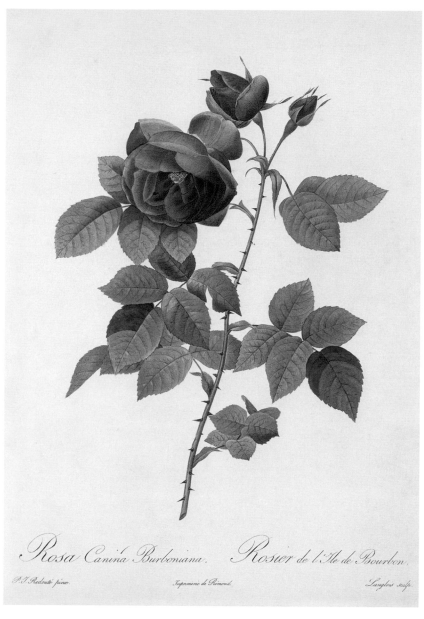

Rosa Canina Burboniana. *Rosier de l'Île de Bourbon.*

P.J. Redouté pinx. Imprimerie de Remond. Langlois sculp.

? ROSA × RAPA BOSC   ROSA × BORBONIANA N. DESP.
? 'Rose d'Amour' | Weiße, gefüllte Glanzrose   Bourbon Rose | Bourbonrose | Rosier Bourbon [et]
Rosier Campanulé à fleurs blanches [et]

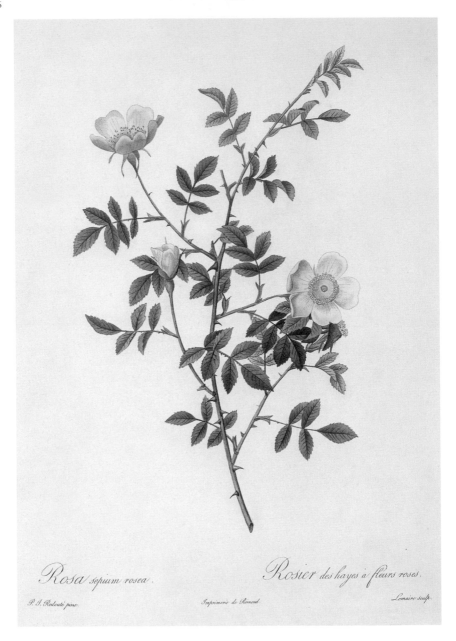

Rosa sepium rosea.

Rosier des hayes à fleurs roses.

P. J. Redouté pinx.

Imprimerie de Remond.

Lemaire sculp.

ROSA AGRESTIS SAVI VAR. *SEPIUM* THUILL.

Grassland Rose | Ackerrosen-Sorte | Rosier des hayes ✤

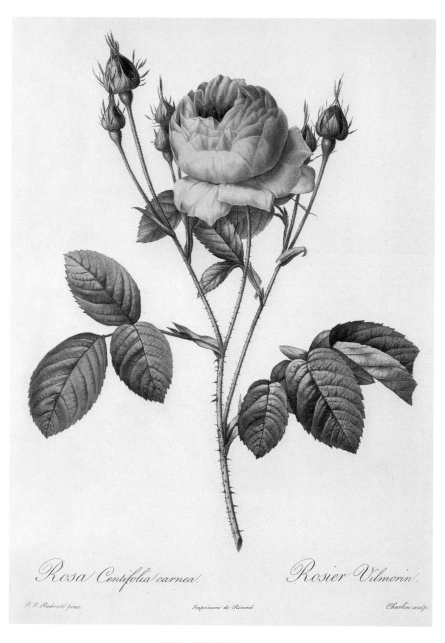

Rosa Centifolia carnea.　　　　*Rosier Vilmorin.*

P. J. Redouté pinx.　　　　Imprimerie de Rémond.　　　　Charlin sculp.

ROSA CENTIFOLIA L. CV.
Variety of Cabbage Rose | Zentifolien-Sorte | Variété du Rosier à centfeuilles ⬸

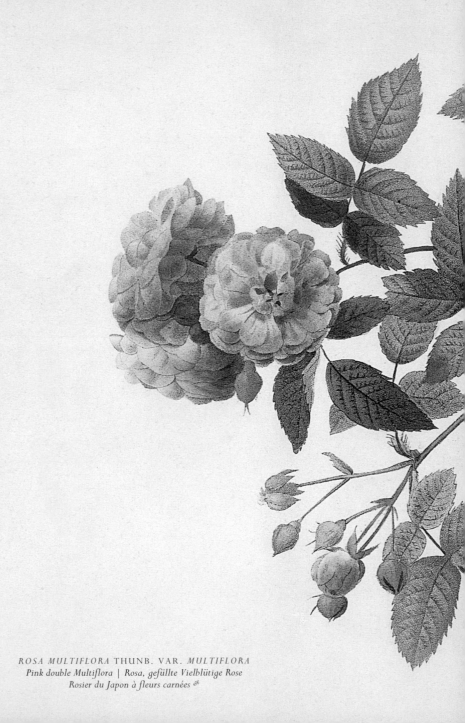

ROSA MULTIFLORA THUNB. VAR. *MULTIFLORA*
Pink double Multiflora | Rosa, gefüllte Vielblütige Rose
Rosier du Japon à fleurs carnées

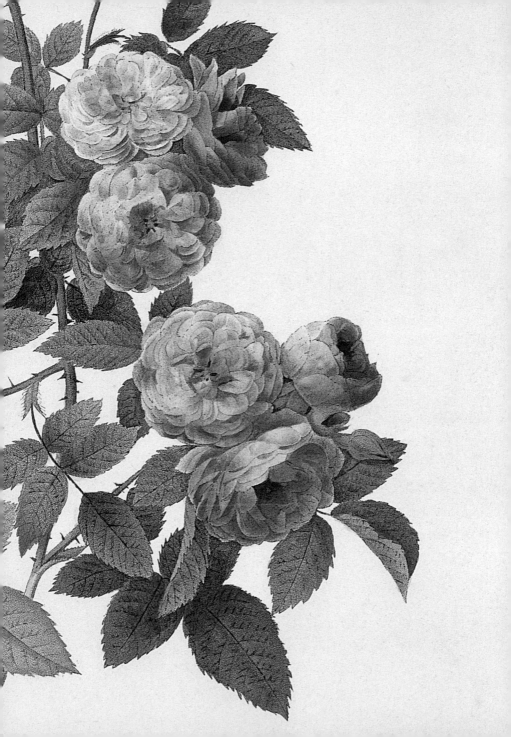

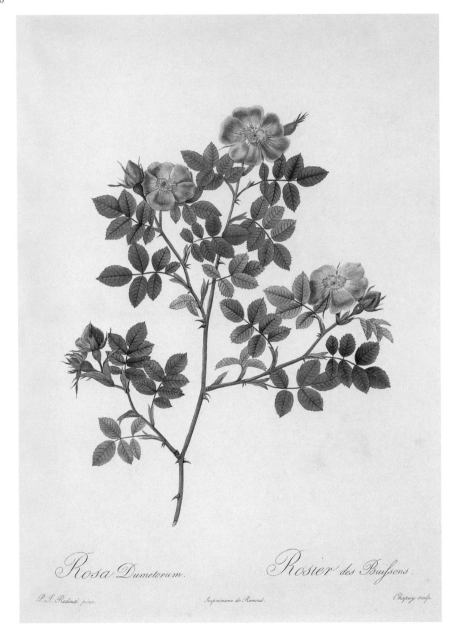

Rosa Dumetorum.   *Rosier des Buissons.*

P.J. Redouté pinx.   Imprimerie de Remond.   Chapuy sculp.

ROSA CORYMBIFERA BORKH.
— | Buschrose | Rosier des Buissons ❧

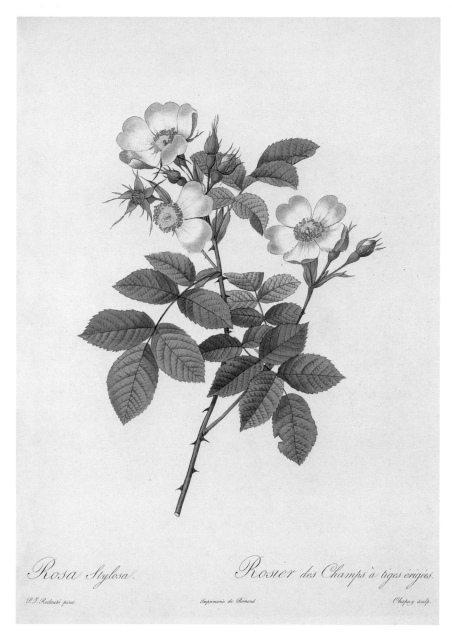

Rosa Stylosa. *Rosier des Champs à tiges érigées.*

P.J. Redouté pinx.   Imprimerie de Remond   Chapuy sculp.

ROSA STYLOSA DESV. VAR. STYLOSA
– | Griffelrose | Rosier à court-style ❧

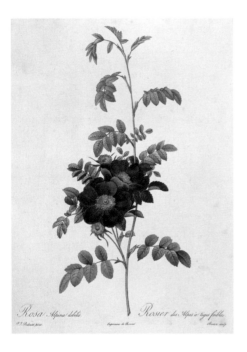

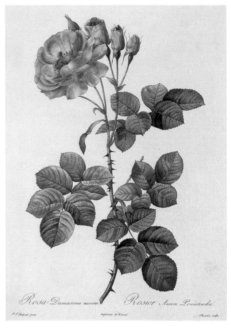

? *ROSA* × *REVERSA* WALDST. & KIT.
Wild hybrid of Alpine Rose
Naturhybride der Alpenheckenrose
Rosier des Alpes – hybride spontané ❧

ROSA × *ALBA* L. 'CELESTE'
White Rose 'Celestial' | *Weiße Rose 'Celeste'*
Rosier blanc 'Celeste' ❧

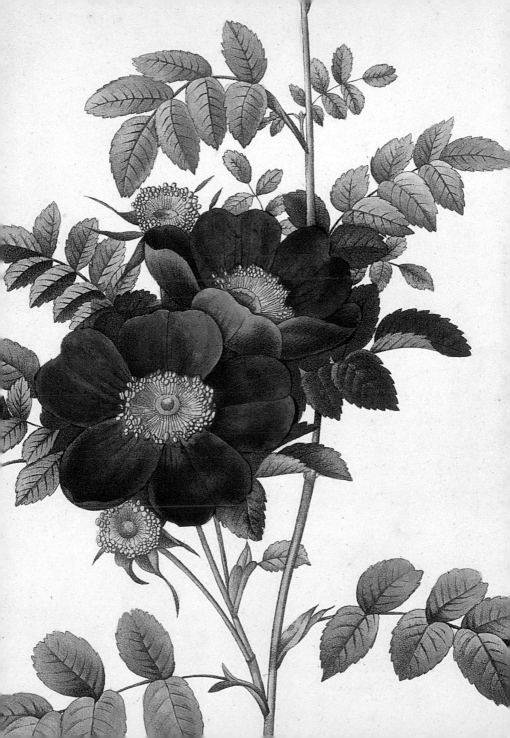

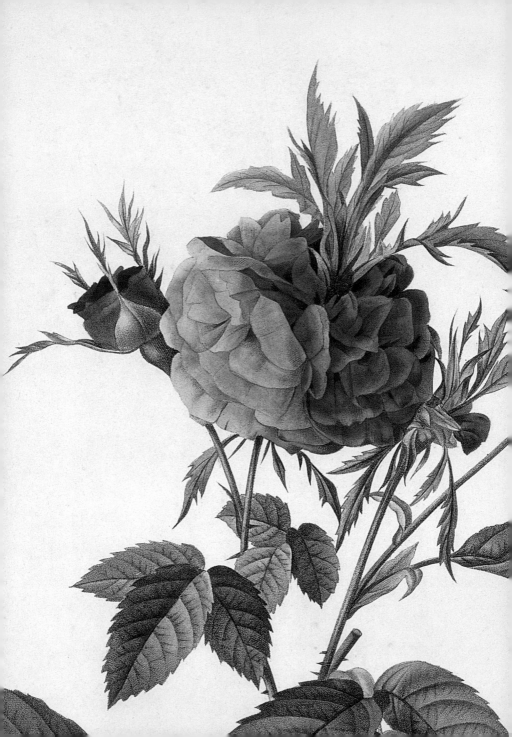

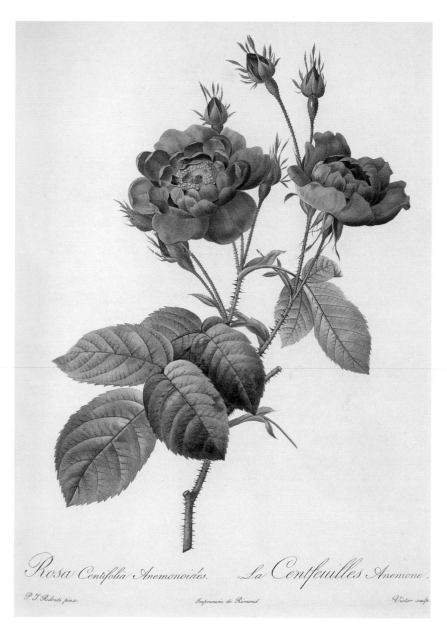

Rosa Centifolia Anemonoides.　　*La Centfeuilles Anemone.*

P. J. Redouté pinx.　　Imprimerie de Rémond　　Victor sculp.

ROSA GALLICA L. CV.
Variety of French Rose | Essigrosen-Sorte
Variété du Rosier de France

ROSA CENTIFOLIA L. 'ANEMONOIDES'
Cabbage Rose 'Anemonoides'
Anemonenblütige Zentifolie
Rosier à centfeuilles à fleurs d'anémone [PJR]

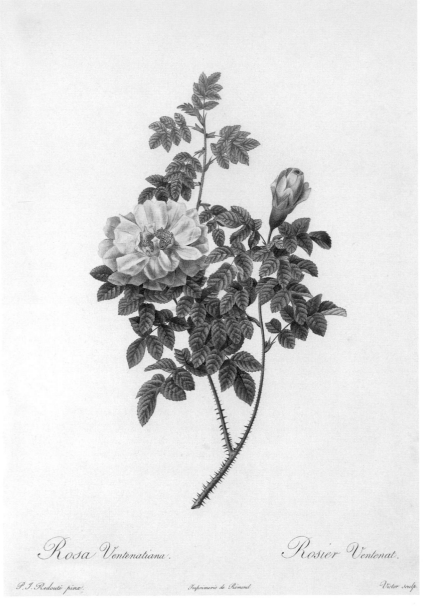

Rosa Ventenatiana.   *Rosier Ventenat.*

P. J. Redouté pinx.   Imprimerie de Rémond   Victor sculp.

ROSA PIMPINELLIFOLIA L. – HYBR.
Burnet Rose hybrid | Bibernellrosen-Hybride
Rosier Pimprenelle hybride ✥

ROSA GALLICA L. × ? ROSA CENTIFOLIA L.
Large-leaved variety of French Rose
Großblättrige Essigrosen-Sorte
Variété du Rosier de France à grandes feuilles ✥

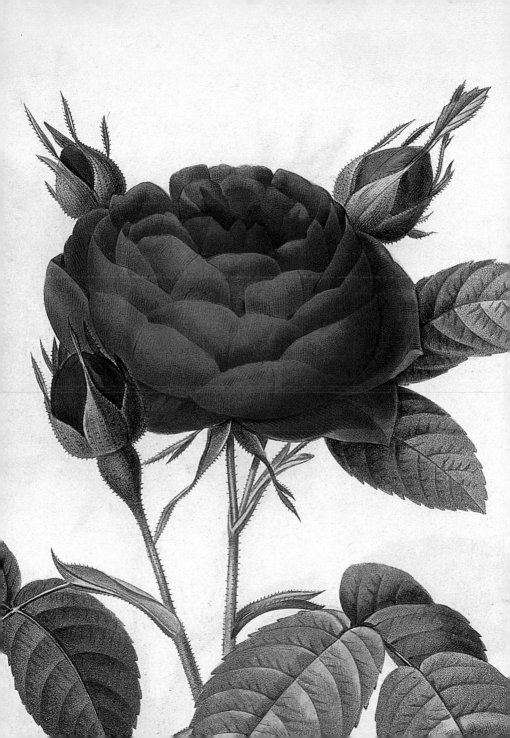

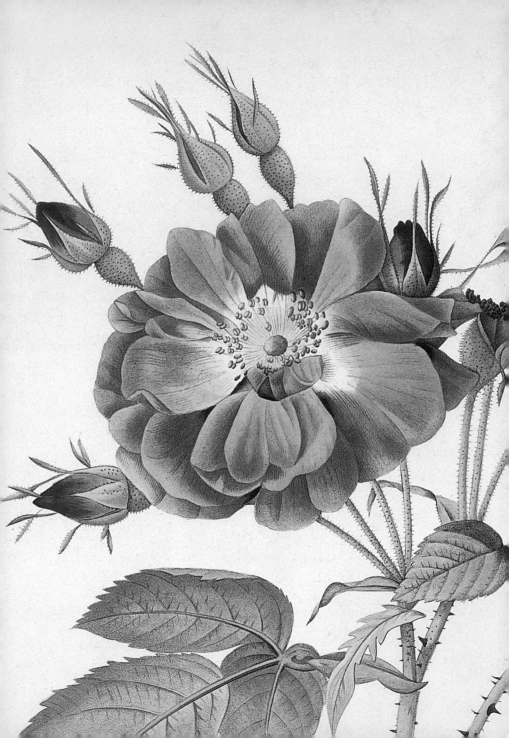

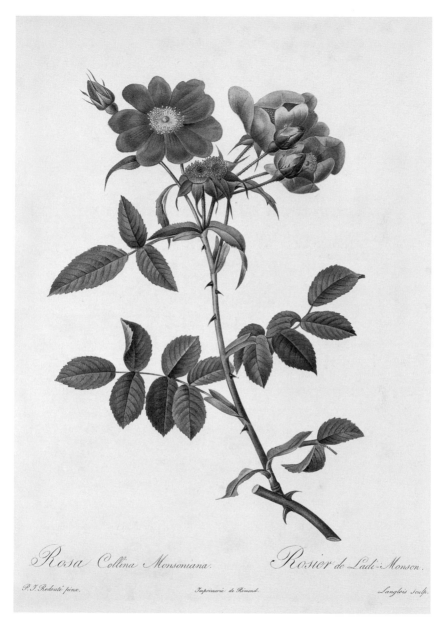

Rosa Collina Monsoniana.   *Rosier de Ladi-Monson.*

P. J. Redouté pinx.   Imprimerie de Rémond.   Langlois sculp.

ROSA TOMENTOSA SMITH CV.
Double variety of Tomentose Rose
Gefüllte Filzrosen-Sorte
Variété du Rosier Tomenteux à fleurs doubles ❧

? *ROSA MONSONIAE* LINDLEY
Rose of Lady Monson | Lady Monson-Rose
Rosier de Lady Monson ❧

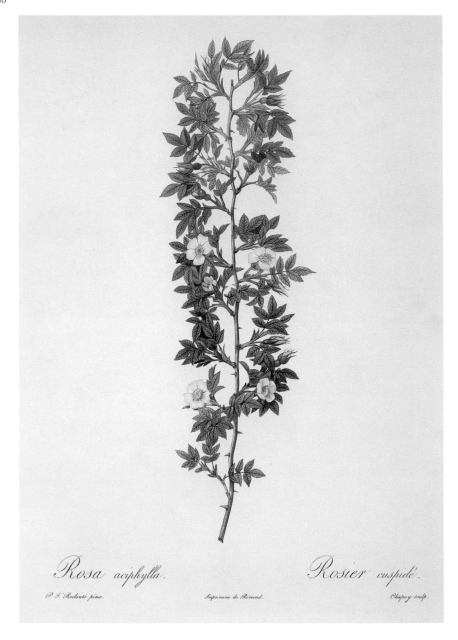

Rosa aciphylla.

Rosier cuspidé.

P. J. Redouté pinx.

Imprimerie de Rémond.

Chapuy sculp.

ROSA CANINA L. VAR. *LUTETIANA* BAKER FOR. *ACIPHYLLA*

Needle-leaved Dog Rose | Nadelblättrige Hundsrose | Variété du Rosier de Chien

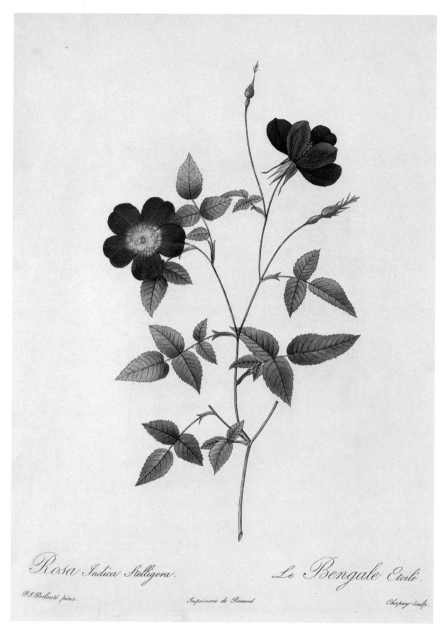

Rosa Indica Stelligera.　　　　*Le Bengale Etoilé.*

P.J.Redouté pinx.　　　Imprimerie de Rémond.　　　Chapuy sculp.

ROSA CHINENSIS JACQ. VAR. SEMPERFLORENS KOEHNE CV.
Variety of Monthly Rose | Monatsrosen-Sorte | Variété du Rosier mensuel

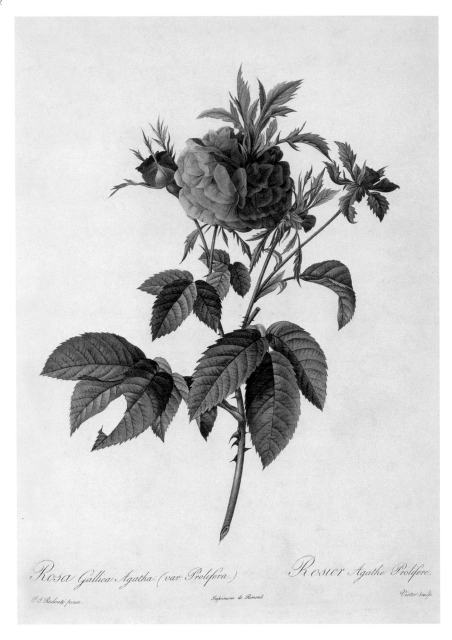

Rosa Gallica Agatha (var. Prolifera.)　　　　*Rosier Agathe Prolifere.*

P. J. Redouté pinx.　　　Imprimerie de Remond.　　　Victor sculp.

ROSA GALLICA L. CV.
Variety of French Rose | Essigrosen-Sorte | Variété du Rosier de France

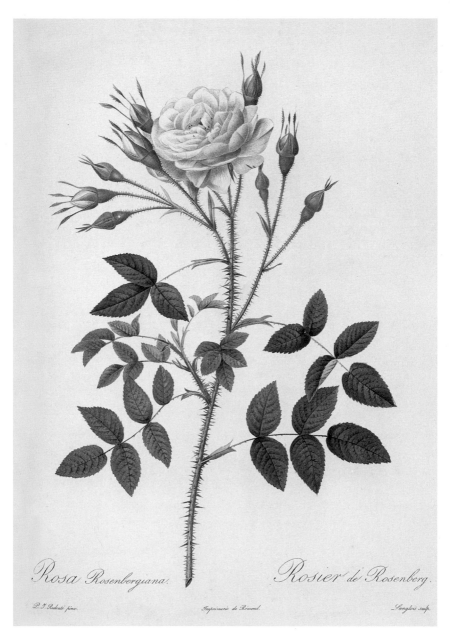

Rosa Rosenbergiana.   *Rosier de Rosenberg.*

P. J. Redouté pinx.   Imprimerie de Rémond.   Langlois sculp.

? *ROSA* × *RAPA* BOSC CV.
— | *Gefüllte Glanzrose* | *Rosier de Rosenberg* [*]

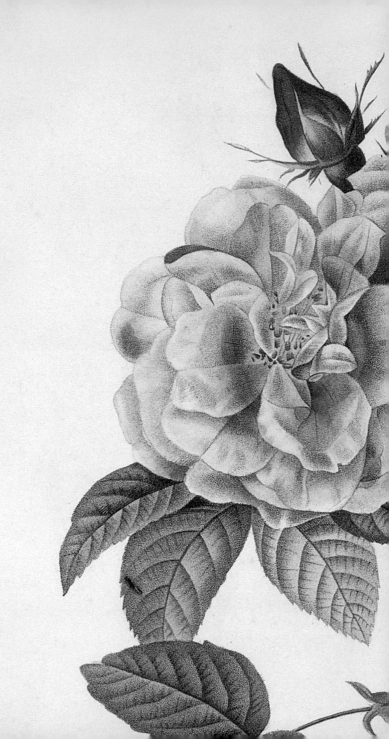

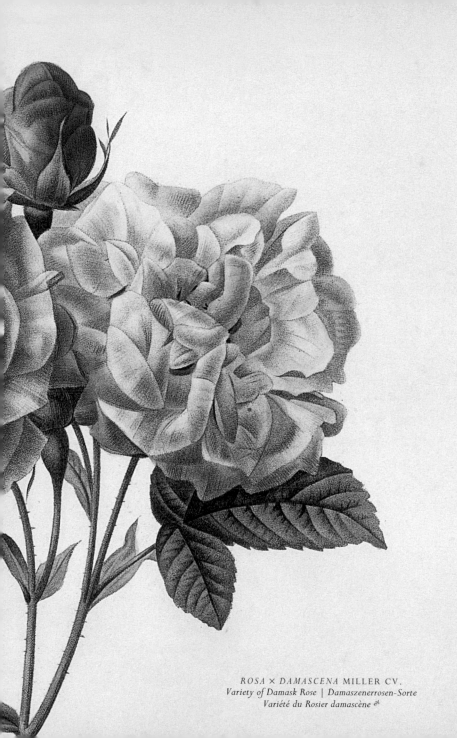

ROSA × *DAMASCENA* MILLER CV.
Variety of Damask Rose | Damaszenerrosen-Sorte
Variété du Rosier damascène

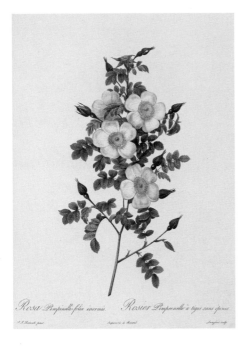

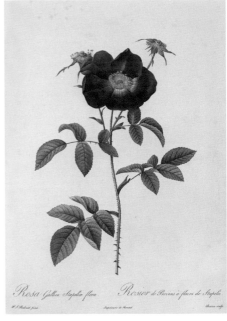

? *ROSA PIMPINELLIFOLIA* L. VAR.
INERMIS DC.
Thornless Burnet Rose | Stachellose Bibernellrose
Rosier Pimprenelle à tiges sans épines 🌹

ROSA GALLICA L. CV.
Stapelia-flowered variety of French Rose
Stapelienblütige Essigrosen-Sorte
Variété du Rosier de France à fleurs de Stapelie 🌹

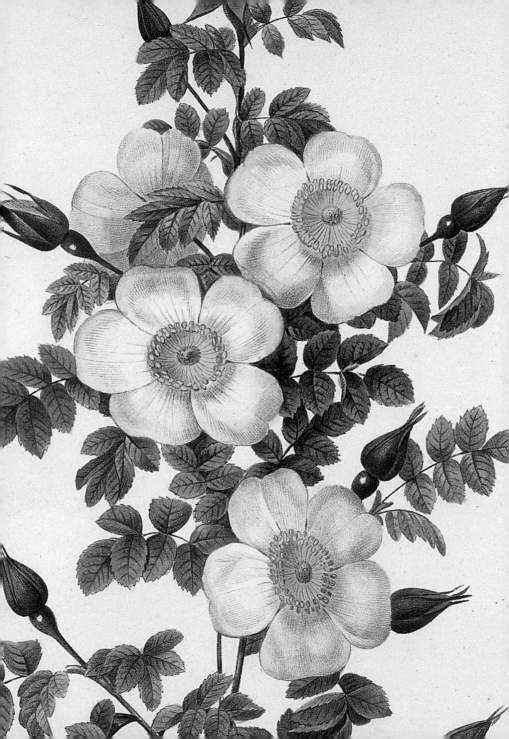

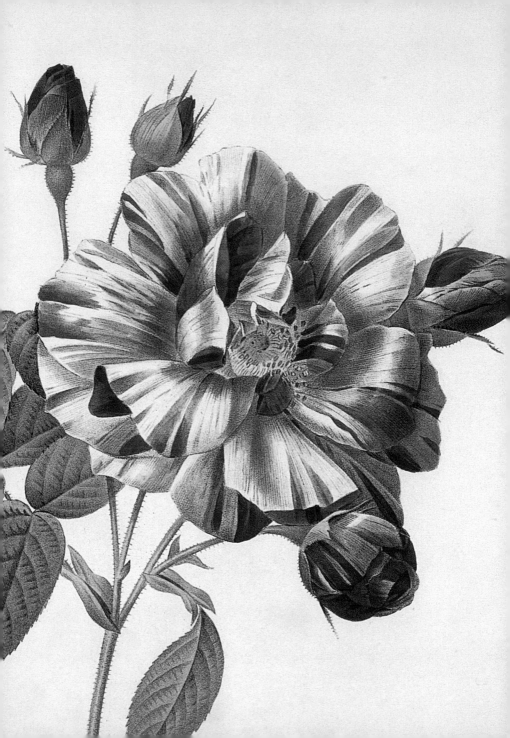

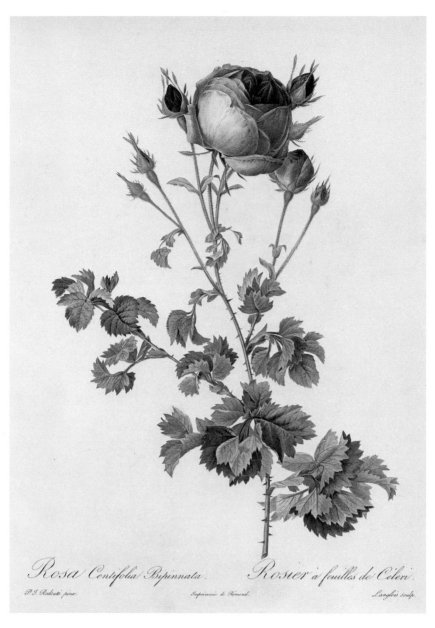

Rosa Centifolia Bipinnata.   *Rosier à feuilles de Céleri.*

P. J. Redouté pinx.   Imprimerie de Rémond.   Langlois sculp.

ROSA GALLICA L. 'VERSICOLOR'
French Rose 'Versicolor'
Panaschiert blühende Essigrose
Rosier de France à fleurs panachées ❦

ROSA CENTIFOLIA L. CV.
Celery-leaved variety of Cabbage Rose
Sellerieblättrige Zentifolien-Sorte
Variété du Rosier à centfeuilles à feuilles de Céleri ❦

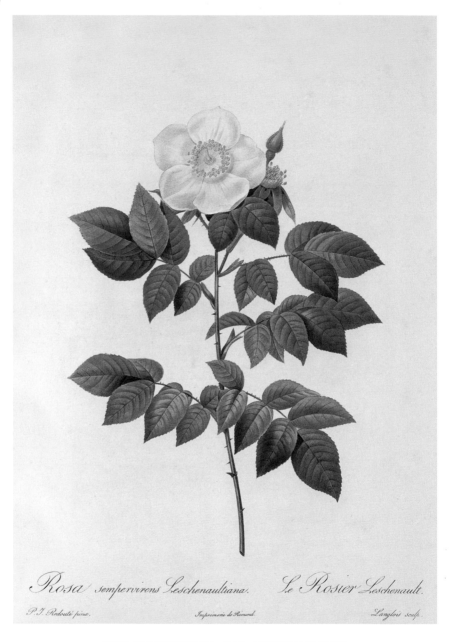

Rosa sempervirens Leschenaultiana.   *Le Rosier Leschenault.*

P. J. Redouté pinx.   Imprimerie de Rémond.   Langlois sculp.

ROSA SEMPERVIRENS L. VAR. LESCHENAULTIANA
Variety of Evergreen Rose | Sorte der Immergrünen Rose | Variété du Rosier à feuilles peristantes

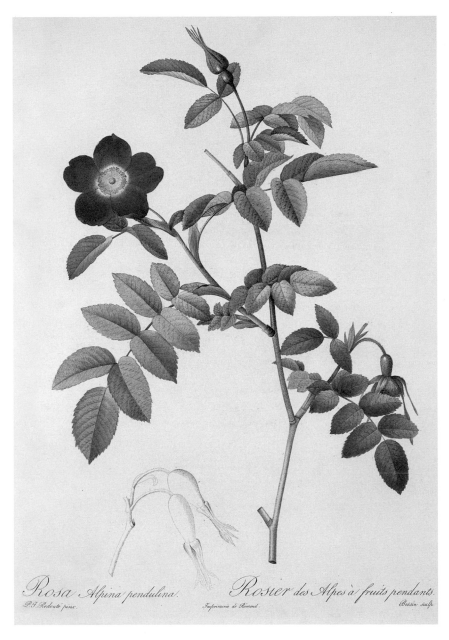

Rosa Alpina pendulina.

Rosier des Alpes à fruits pendants.

P.J.Redouté pinx.

Imprimerie de Rémond.

Bessin sculp.

ROSA PENDULINA L. VAR. PENDULINA

Alpine Rose | Alpenheckenrose | Rosier des Alpes

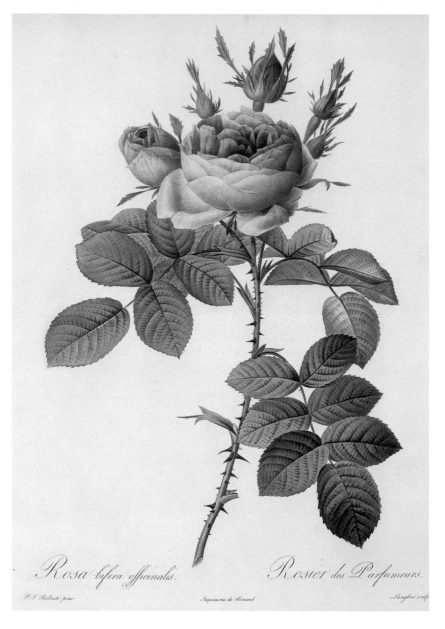

Rosa bifera officinalis.   *Rosier des Parfumeurs.*

P. J. Redouté pinx.   Imprimerie de Rémond.   Langlois sculp.

ROSA × BIFERA PERS.
Autumn Damask Rose | Herbst-Damaszenerrose
Rosier damascène d'Automne

ROSA RUGOSA THUNB.
Japanese Rose | Kartoffelrose
Rosier à feuilles rugueuses

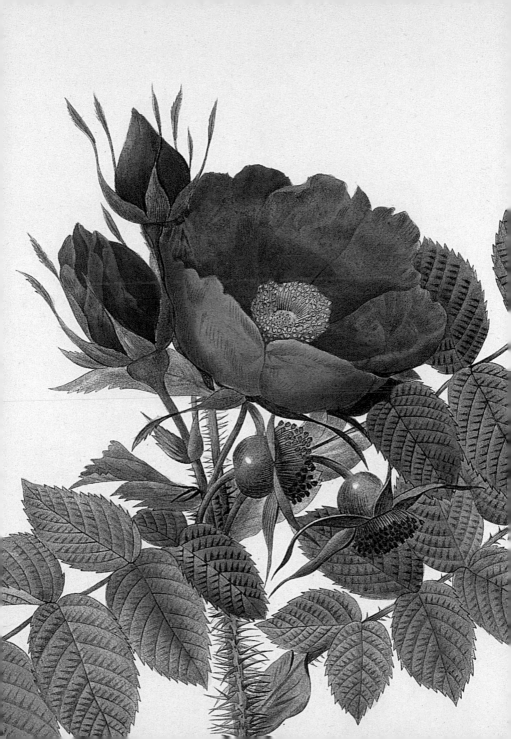

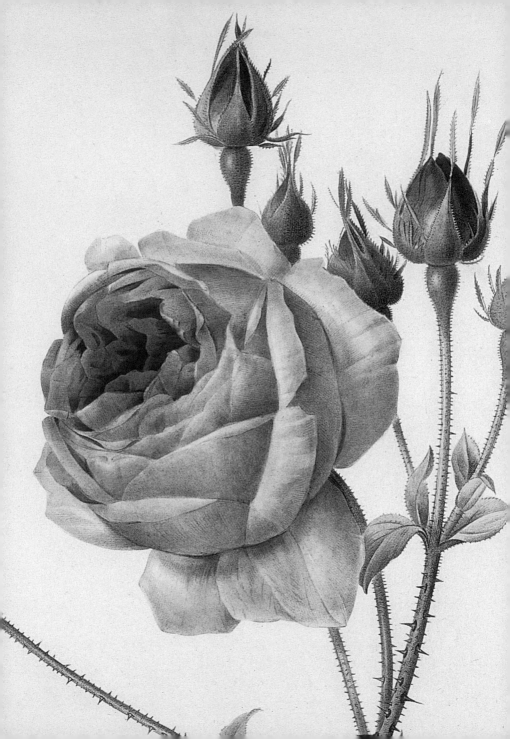

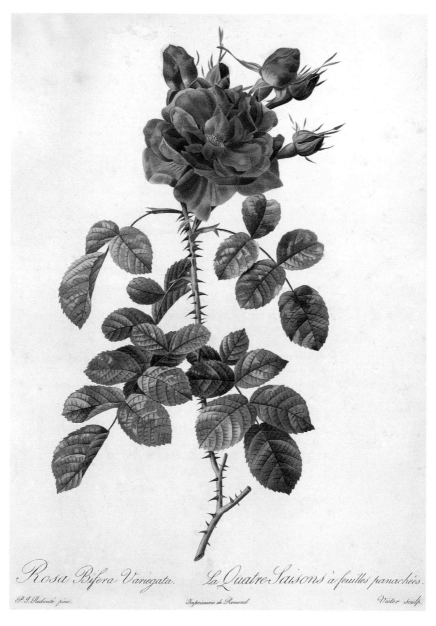

Rosa Bifera Variegata.   *La Quatre Saisons à feuilles panachées.*

P.J. Redouté pinx.   Imprimerie de Remond   Victor Sculp.

ROSA CENTIFOLIA L. 'BULLATA'
Lettuce-leaved Cabbage Rose | Salatrose
Rosier à feuilles de Laitue

ROSA × BIFERA PERS. CV.
Variegated variety of Autumn Damask Rose
Panaschiertblättrige Herbst-Damaszenerrose
Variété du Rosier damascène d'Automne panaché

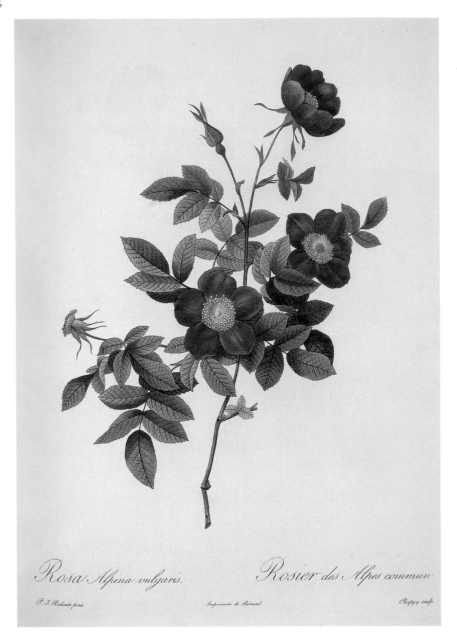

Rosa Alpina vulgaris.　　　　*Rosier des Alpes commun.*

P. J. Redouté pinx.　　　　Imprimerie de Rémond.　　　　Chapuy sculp.

ROSA PENDULINA L. VAR. PENDULINA
Alpine Rose | Alpenheckenrose | Rosier des Alpes ❧

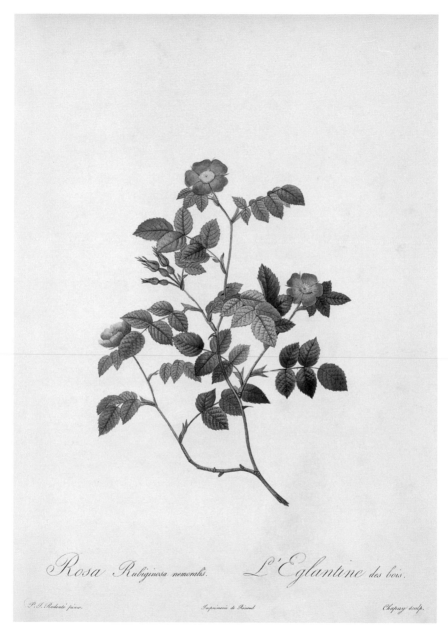

Rosa Rubiginosa nemoralis. *L'Eglantine des bois.*

P. J. Redouté pinx. Imprimerie de Rémond Chapuy sculp.

ROSA MICRANTHA BORRER VAR. *MICRANTHA*
Small flowered Eglantine | Kleinblütige Rose | Eglantier des bois ❧

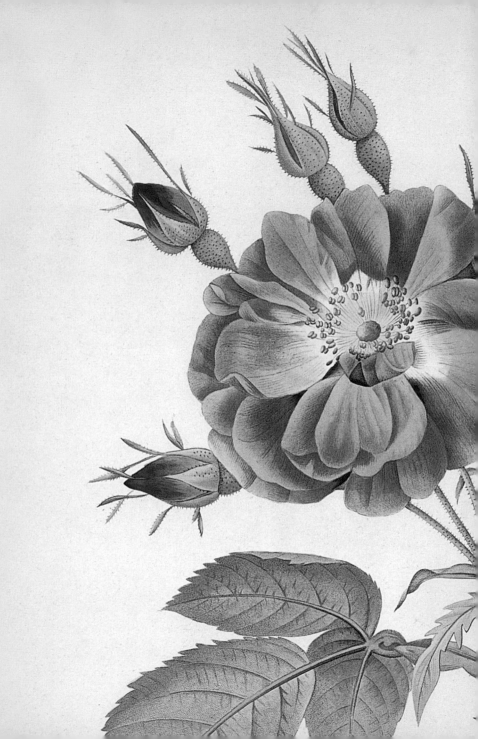

ROSA TOMENTOSA SMITH CV.
Double variety of Tomentose Rose | Gefüllte Filzrosen-Sorte
Variété du Rosier Tomenteux à fleurs doubles ❧

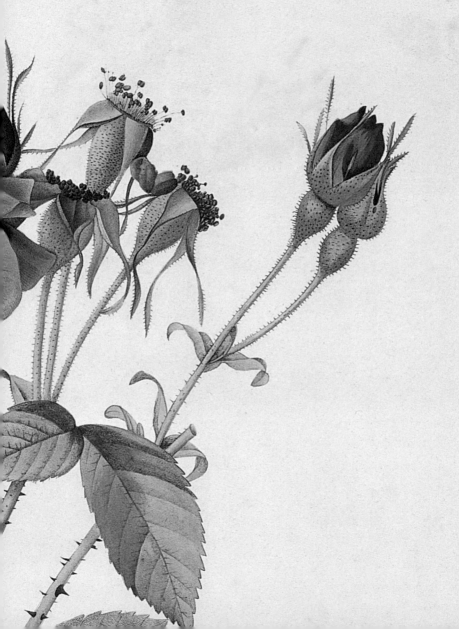

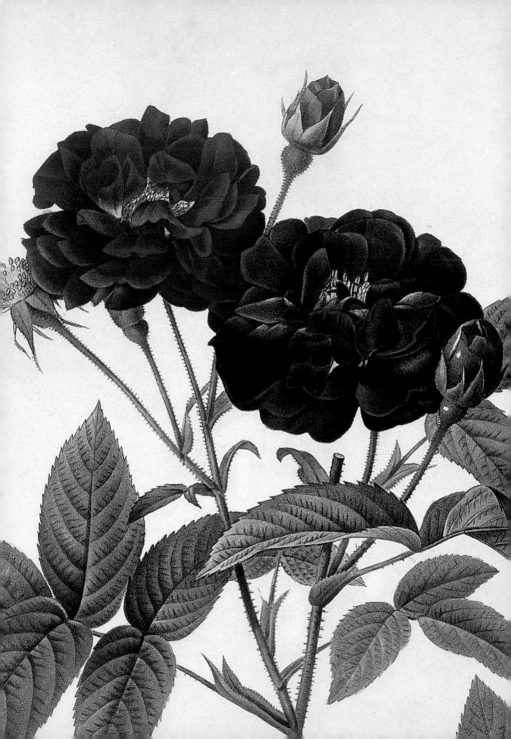

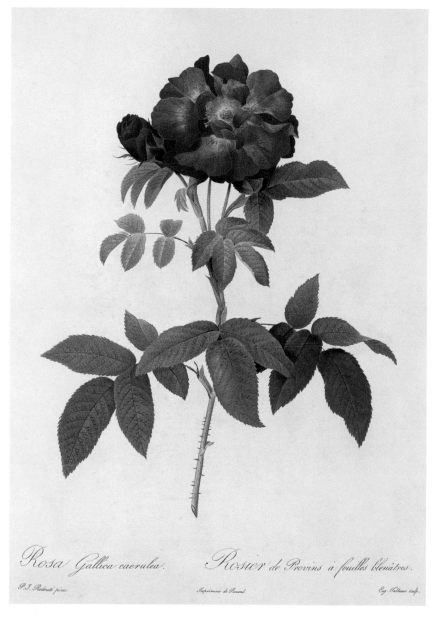

Rosa Gallica caerulea.   *Rosier de Provins à feuilles bleuâtres.*

P.J. Redouté pinx.   Imprimerie de Remond.   Eng. Talbaux sculp.

ROSA GALLICA L. CV. ? 'TUSCANY'
Variety of French Rose ? 'Tuscany' ?
Essigrosen-Sorte ? 'Tuscany' ?
Variété du Rosier de France [Fra]

ROSA GALLICA L. CV.
Variety of French Rose | Essigrosen-Sorte
Variété du Rosier de France [ed]

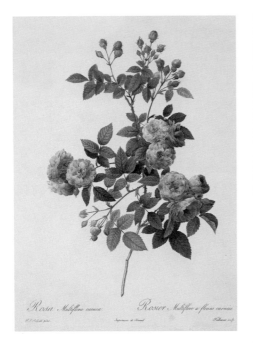

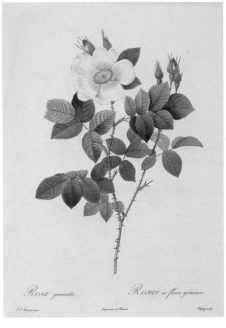

ROSA MULTIFLORA THUNB. VAR.
MULTIFLORA
Pink double Multiflora | Rosa, gefüllte Vielblütige Rose
Rosier du Japon à fleurs carnées ❦

ROSA × POLLINIANA SPRENGEL ❦

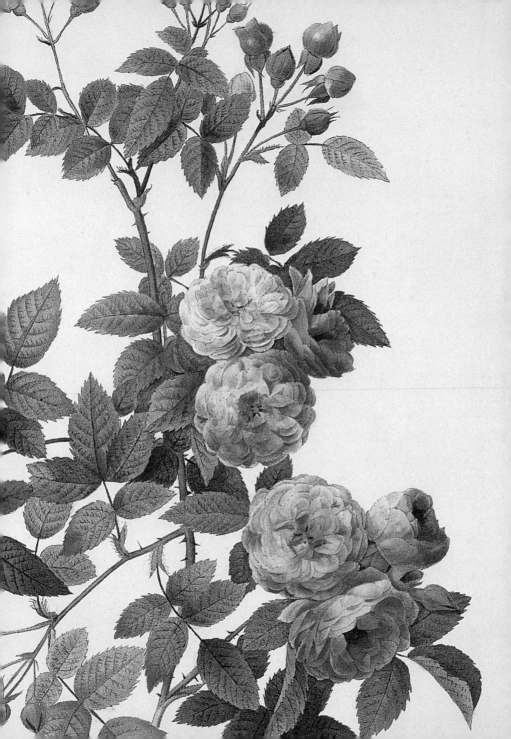

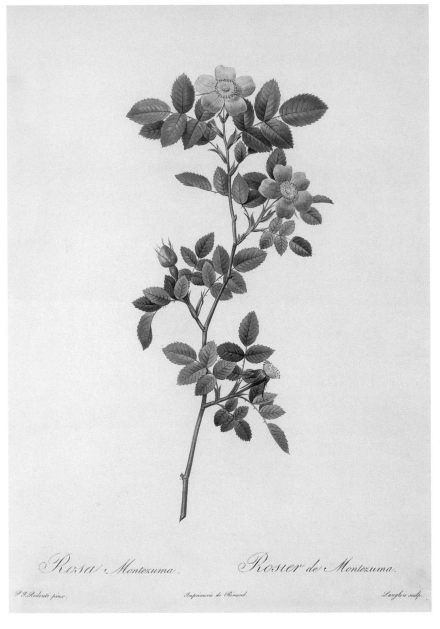

Rosa Montezuma. *Rosier de Montezuma.*

P.J.Redouté pinx. Imprimerie de Rémond. Langlois sculp.

ROSA CANINA L. VAR. *MONTEZUMAE*
HUMB. & BONPL.
Montezuma Rose | Montezuma-Rose
Rosier de Montezuma ❧

ROSA TOMENTOSA SMITH CV.
Semi-double variety of Tomentose Rose
Halbgefüllte Filzrosen-Sorte
Variété du Rosier Tomenteux à fleurs semi-doubles ❧

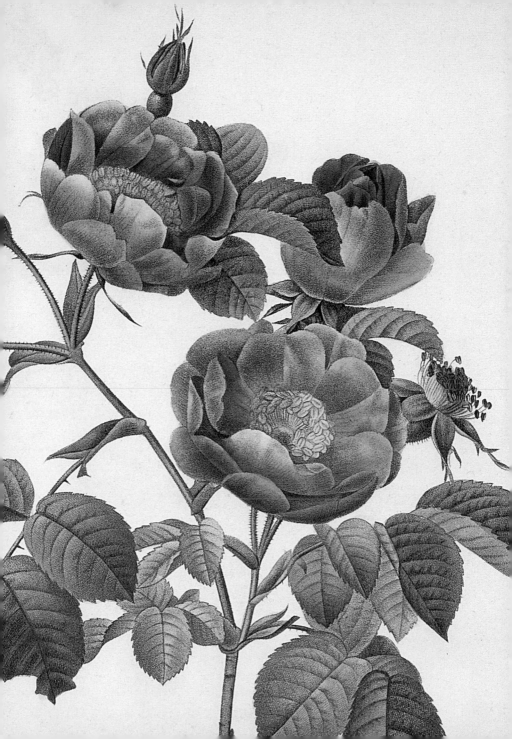

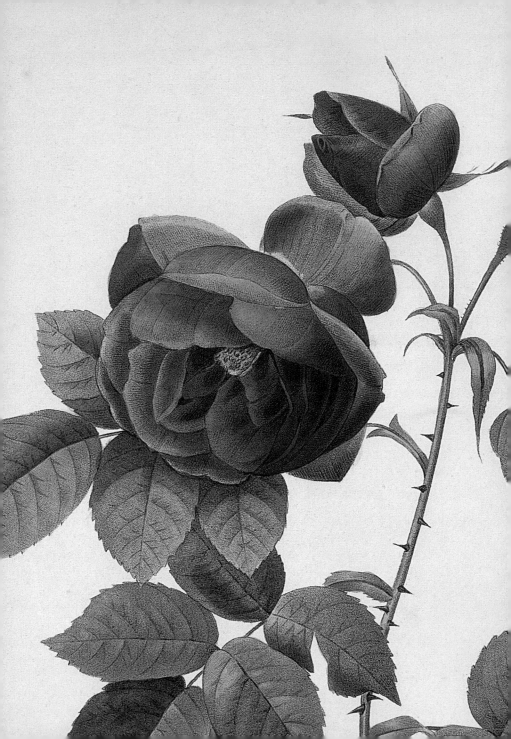

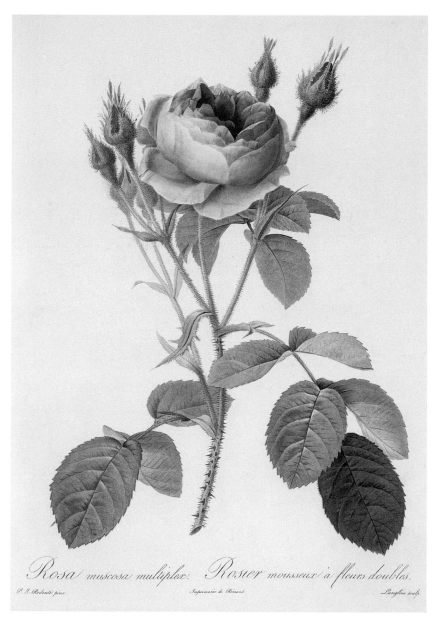

Rosa muscosa multiplex. Rosier mousseux à fleurs doubles.

P. J. Redouté pinx.   Imprimerie de Rémond   Langlois sculp.

ROSA × BORBONIANA N. DESP.
Bourbon Rose | Bourbonrose | Rosier Bourbon

ROSA CENTIFOLIA L. 'MUSCOSA'
Double Moss Rose | Gefüllte Moosrose
Rosier mousseux à fleurs doubles

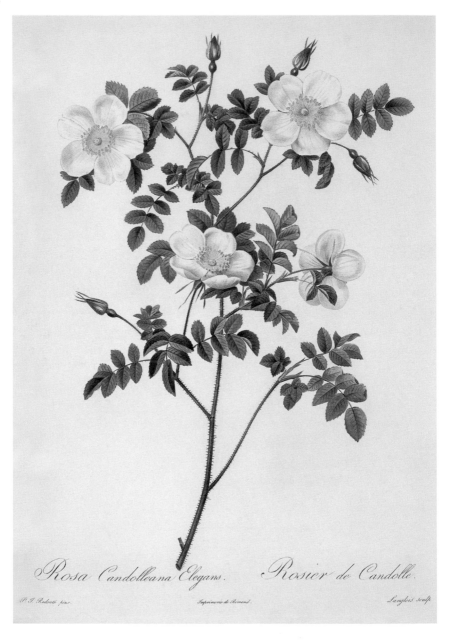

Rosa Candolleana Elegans.   *Rosier de Candolle.*

P. J. Redouté pinx.   Imprimerie de Rémond.   Langlois sculp.

ROSA × *REVERSA* WALDST. & KIT.
De Candolle Rose | De Candolle-Rose | Rosier de Candolle ❦

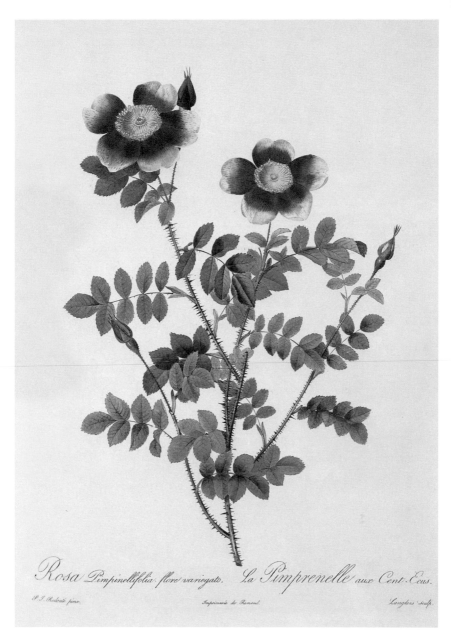

Rosa Pimpinellifolia flore variegato. *La Pimprenelle aux Cent-Ecus.*

P. J. Redouté pinx.   Imprimerie de Remond.   Langlois sculp.

ROSA PIMPINELLIFOLIA L. VAR. CIPHIANA
Variegated flowering variety of Burnet Rose | Panaschiertblütige Bibernellrosen-Sorte
Variété du Rosier Pimprenelle à fleurs panachées

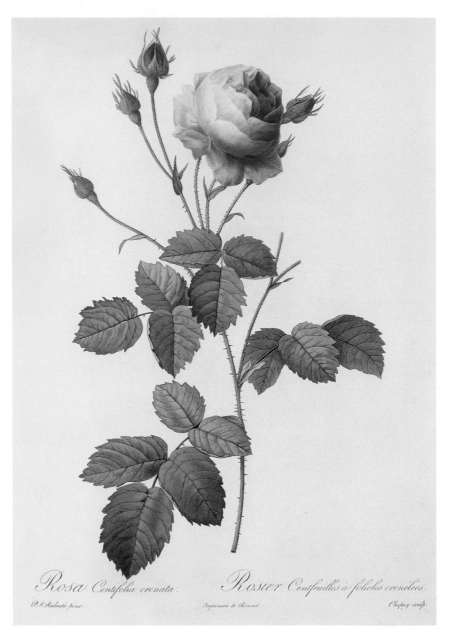

Rosa Centifolia crenata.   *Rosier* Centfeuilles à folioles crenelées.

P.J Redouté pinx.   Imprimerie de Remond   Chapuy sculp.

ROSA CENTIFOLIA L. CV.
Variety of Cabbage Rose | Zentifolien-Sorte | Variété du Rosier à centfeuilles &

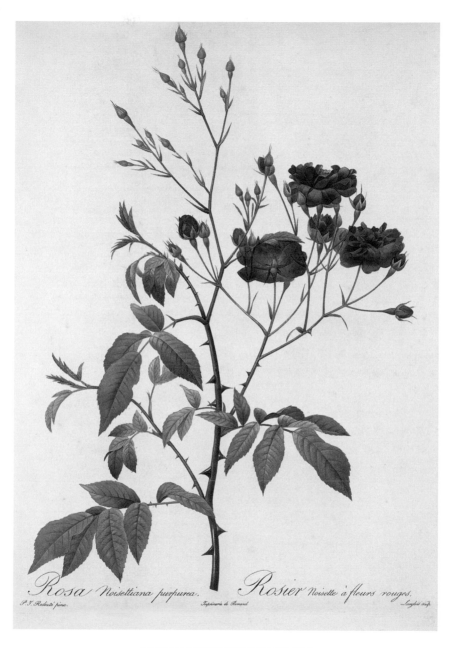

Rosa Noisettiana purpurea.

Rosier Noisette à fleurs rouges.

P. J. Redouté pinx.   Imprimerie de Remond   Langlois sculp.

? *ROSA* × *L'HERITIERANEA* THORY
Boursault Rose | Boursault-Rose | Rosier de Boursault &

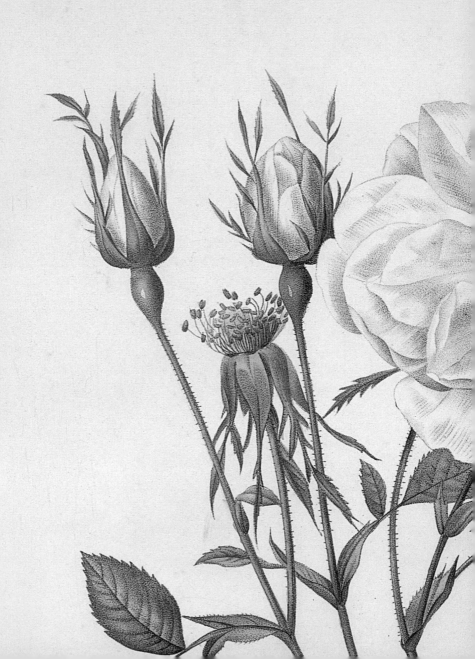

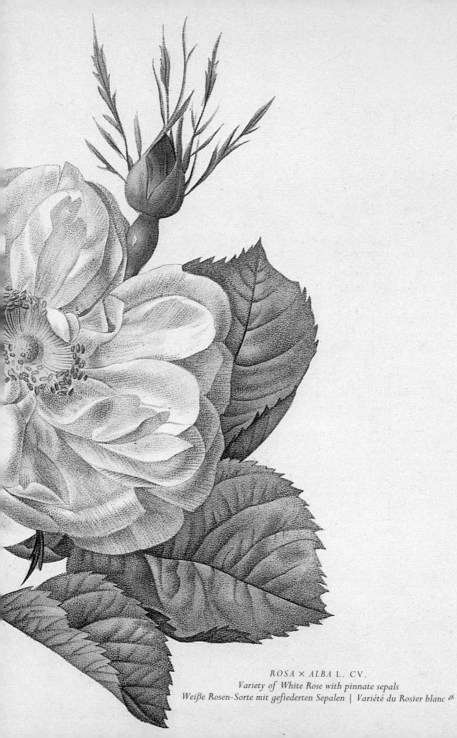

ROSA × ALBA L. CV.
Variety of White Rose with pinnate sepals
Weiße Rosen-Sorte mit gefiederten Sepalen | Variété du Rosier blanc

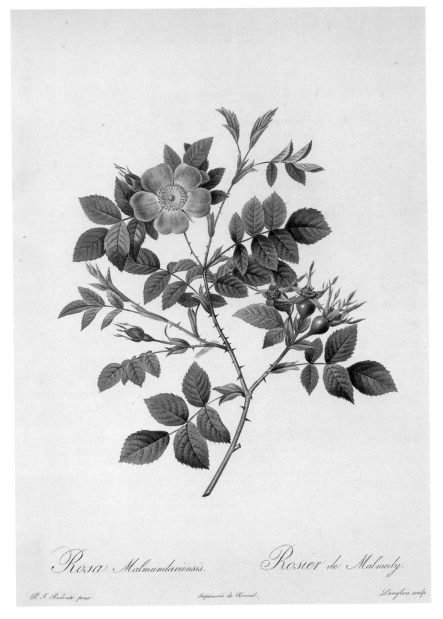

Rosa Malmundariensis.

Rosier de Malmedy.

P. J. Redouté pinx.

Imprimerie de Rémond.

Langlois sculp.

ROSA DUMALIS BECHSTEIN VAR.
MALMUNDARIENSIS
Malmedy Rose | Malmedy-Rose
Rosier de Malmedy ❧

ROSA HYBRIDA 'DUCHESS OF
PORTLAND'
Portland Rose 'Duchess of Portland
Portland-Rose 'Duchess of Portland'
Rosier de Portland 'Duchess of Portland' ❧

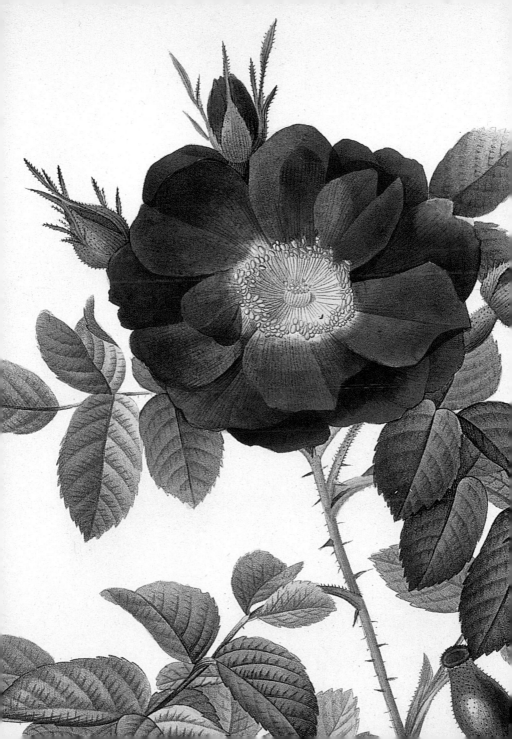

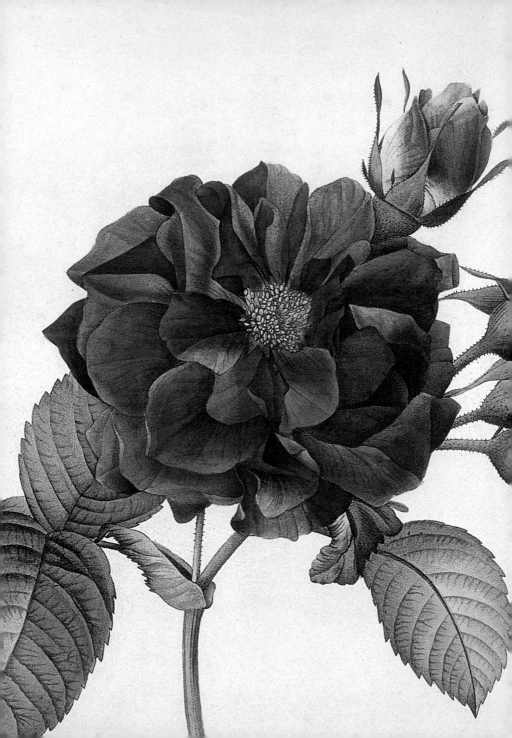

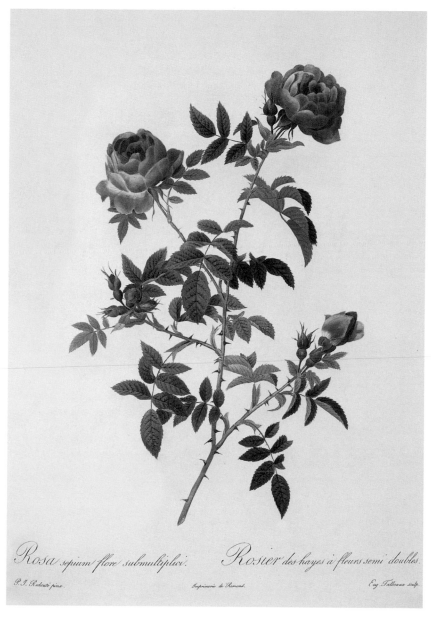

Rosa sepium flore submultiplici.　　*Rosier des hayes à fleurs semi doubles.*

P.J. Redouté pinx.　　　Imprimerie de Rémond.　　　Eug. Tolleau sculp.

ROSA 'FRANCOFURTANA'
'Empress Josephine' | 'Impératrice Joséphine'
'Impératrice Joséphine'

ROSA AGRESTIS SAVI CV.
Semi-double variety of Grassland Rose
Halbgefüllte Ackerrosen-Sorte
Rosier des hayes à fleurs semi-doubles

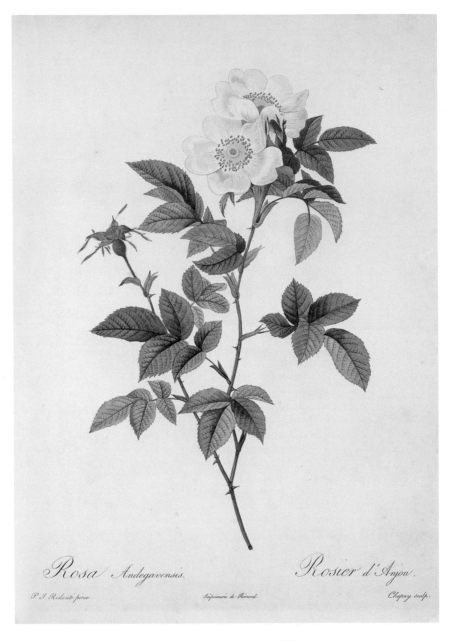

Rosa Andegavensis.   *Rosier d'Anjou.*

P. J. Redouté pinx.   Imprimerie de Rémond.   Chapuy sculp.

ROSA CANINA L. VAR. ANDEGAVENSIS BAST.
Anjou Rose | Anjou-Rose | Rosier d'Anjou [96]

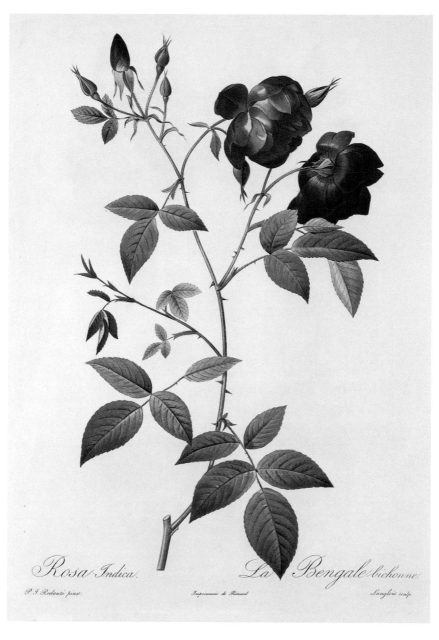

Rosa Indica. — *La Bengale bichonne.*

P. J. Redouté pinx. — Imprimerie de Rémond — Langlois sculp.

ROSA CHINENSIS JACQ. 'MULTIPETALA'
Double variety of China Rose | Gefüllte Chinarosen-Sorte | Rosier de Chine à fleurs doubles

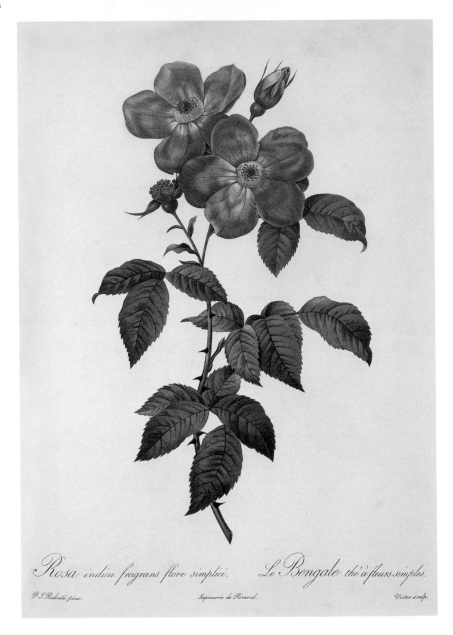

Rosa indica fragrans flore simplici.   *Le Bengale thé à fleurs simples.*

P. J. Redouté pinx.   Imprimerie de Rémond.   Victor sculp.

ROSA × *ODORATA* SWEET CV.   *ROSA CENTIFOLIA* L. 'ANEMONOIDES'
Single variety of Tea Rose   Cabbage Rose 'Anemonoides'
Einfache Teerosen-Sorte   Anemonenblütige Zentifolie
Variété du Rosier à odeur de thé à fleurs simples   Rosier à centfeuilles à fleurs d'anémone

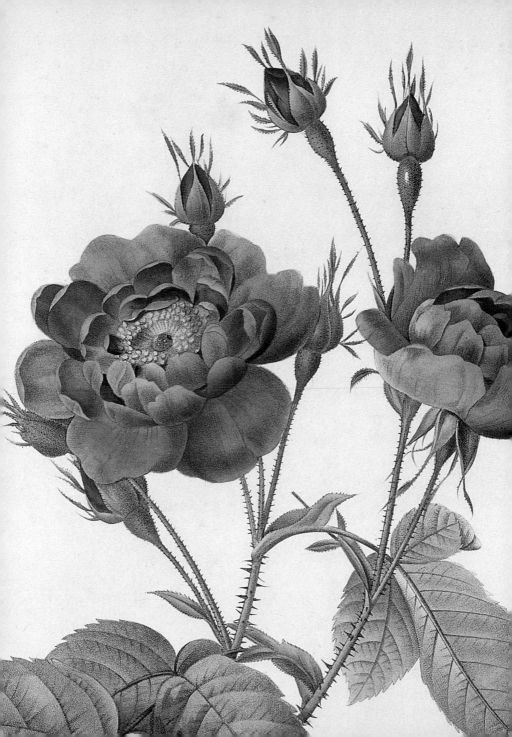

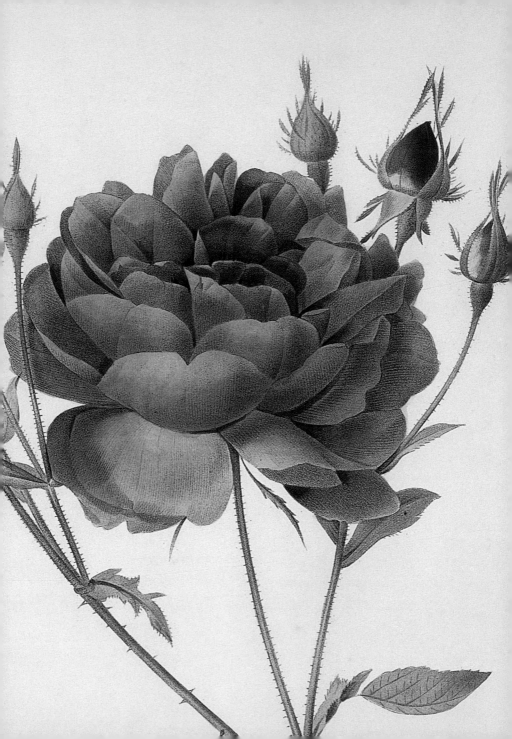

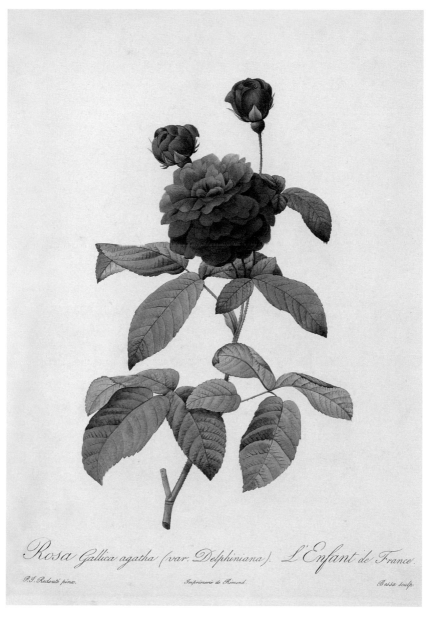

Rosa Gallica agatha (var. Delphiniana). L'Enfant de France.

P.J. Redouté pinx.   Imprimerie de Rémond.   Bessa sculp.

ROSA CENTIFOLIA L. CV.	*ROSA GALLICA* L. CV.
Variety of Cabbage Rose | Zentifolien-Sorte	Variety of French Rose | Essigrosen-Sorte
Variété du Rosier à centfeuilles *∞*	Variété du Rosier de France *∞*

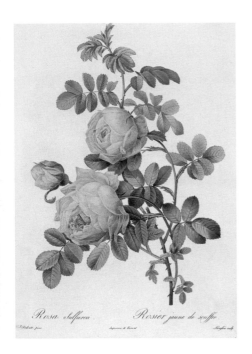

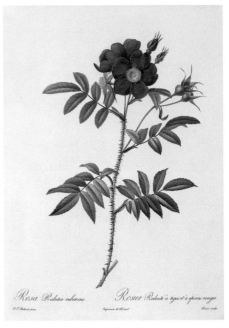

ROSA HEMISPHAERICA HERRM.
Sulphur Rose | Schwefelrose
Rosier à fleurs jaune soufre ❦

ROSA VILLOSA L. × ROSA PIMPINELLIFOLIA L.
Redouté Rose with red stems and prickles
Rotstielige Redouté-Rose
Rosier Redouté à tiges et à épines rouges ❦

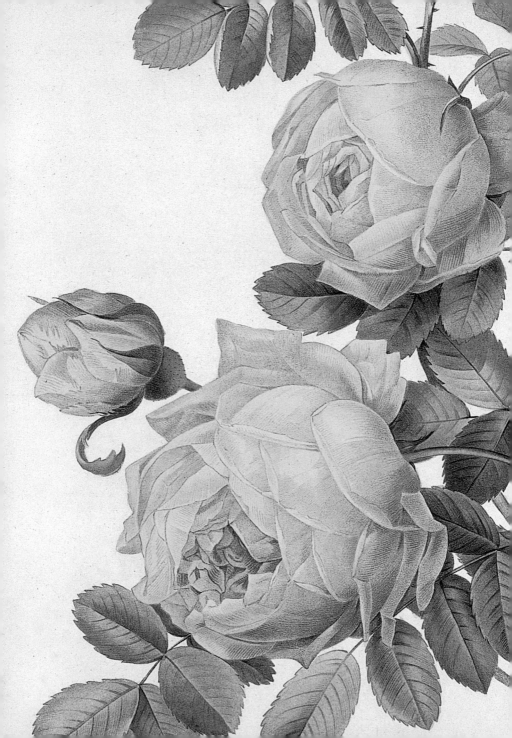

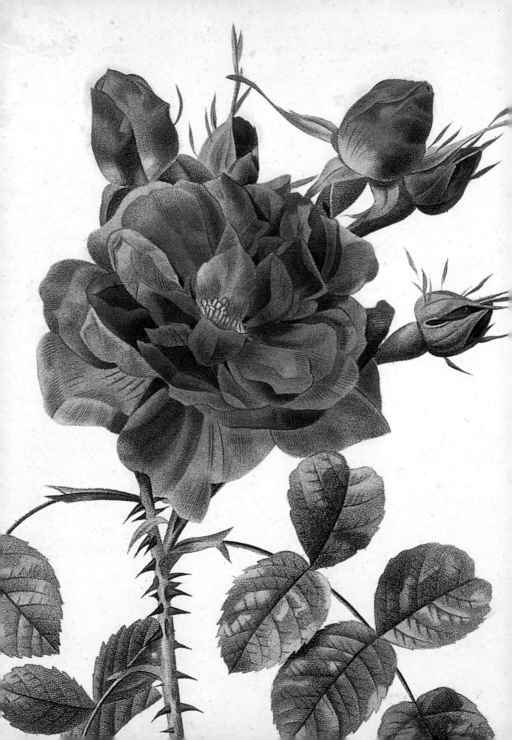

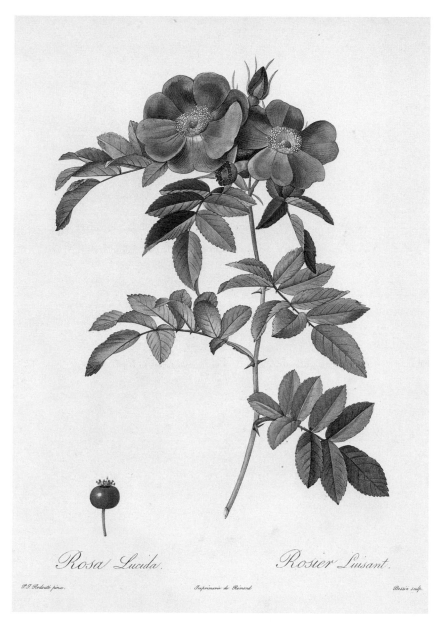

Rosa Lucida.　　　*Rosier Luisant.*

P.J. Redouté pinx.　　　Imprimerie de Rémond　　　Bessin sculp.

ROSA × BIFERA PERS. CV.
Variegated variety of Autumn Damask Rose
Panaschiertblättrige Herbst-Damaszenerrose
Variété du Rosier damascène d'Automne panaché ↙

ROSA VIRGINIANA HERRM.
Virginia Rose | Glanzrose
Rosier à feuilles luisantes ↙

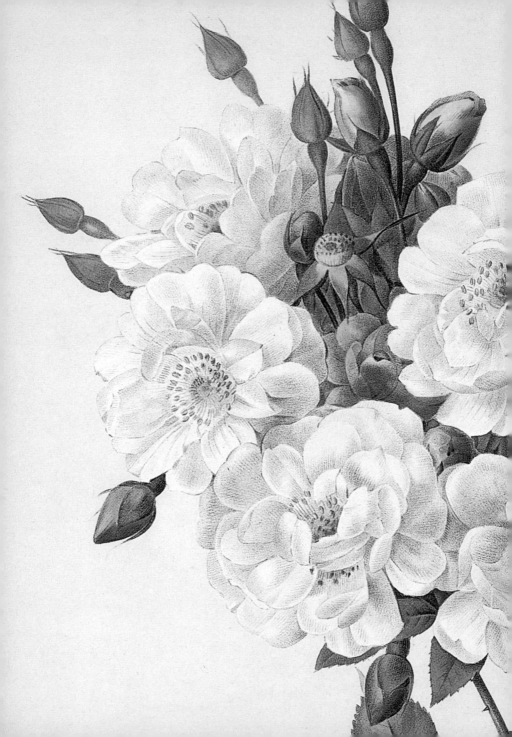

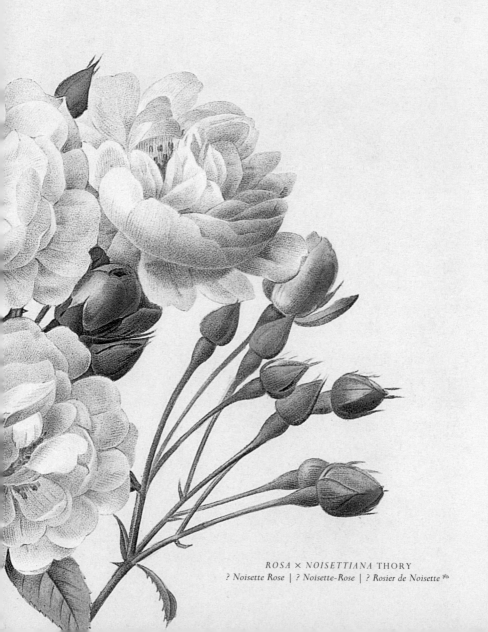

ROSA × *NOISETTIANA* THORY
? Noisette Rose | ? Noisette-Rose | ? Rosier de Noisette ¹ᵃ

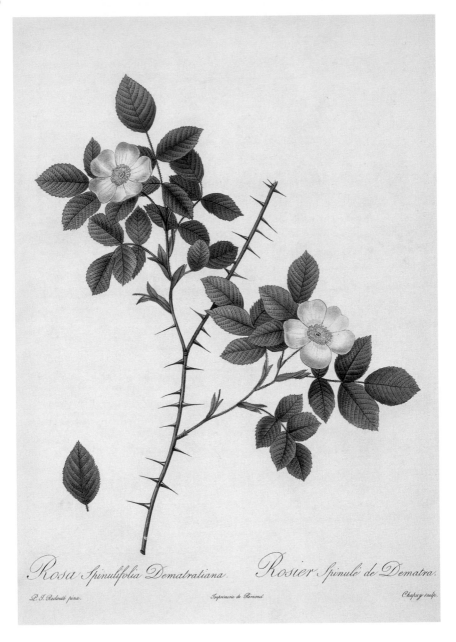

Rosa Spinulifolia Dematratiana.   *Rosier Spinulé de Dematra.*

P. J. Redouté pinx.   Imprimerie de Remond.   Chapuy sculp.

ROSA × SPINULIFOLIA DEMATRA
Wild hybrid of Alpine Rose | Naturhybride der Alpenrose | Rosier des Alpes — hybride spontané ❦

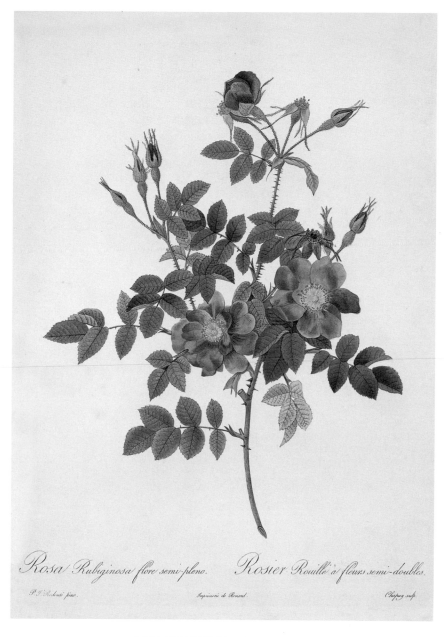

Rosa Rubiginosa flore semi-pleno.   *Rosier Rouille à fleurs semi-doubles.*

P.J. Redouté pinx.   Imprimerie de Remond.   Chapuy sculp.

ROSA RUBIGINOSA L. 'SEMIPLENA'
Semi-double Sweet Briar | Halbgefüllte Weinrose | Rosier rubigineux à fleurs semi-doubles

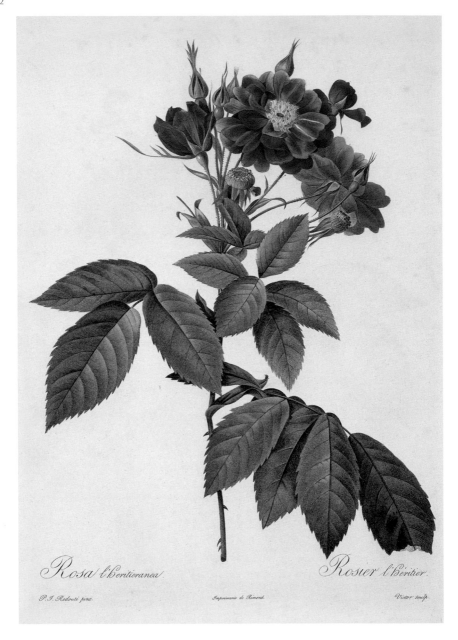

Rosa l'heritieranea.   *Rosier l'heritier.*

P. J. Redouté pinx.   Imprimerie de Remond.   Victor sculp.

ROSA × *L'HERITIERANEA* THORY
Boursault Rose | Boursault-Rose | Rosier de Boursault

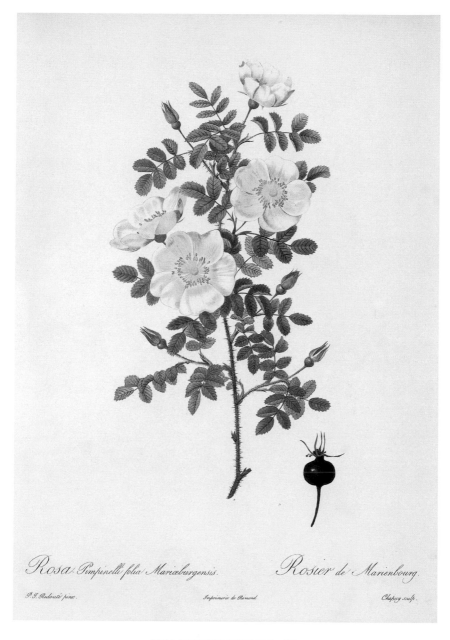

Rosa Pimpinellifolia Mariæburgensis. *Rosier de Marienbourg.*

P.J. Redouté pinx. Imprimerie de Remond Chapuy sculp.

ROSA PIMPINELLIFOLIA L. CV.
Burnet Rose of Marienburg | Bibernellrose 'Marienburg' | Rosier Pimprenelle de Marienbourg [183]

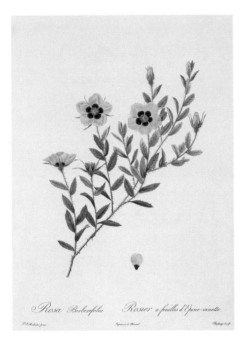

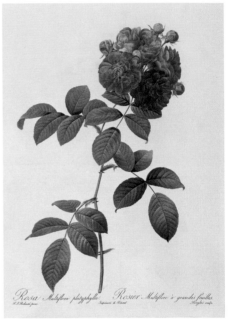

Rosa Berberifolia — *Rosier a feuilles d'Épine-vinette*

Rosa Multiflora platyphylla — *Rosier Multiflore à grandes feuilles*

ROSA PERSICA MICHAUX

Barberry Rose | Persische Rose | Rosier de Perse

ROSA MULTIFLORA THUNB. VAR.
PLATYPHYLLA REHDER ET WILSON
'SEVEN SISTERS ROSE'

Multiflora 'Seven Sisters Rose' | Vielblütige Rose 'Seven Sisters Rose' | Rosier du Japon 'Seven Sisters Rose'

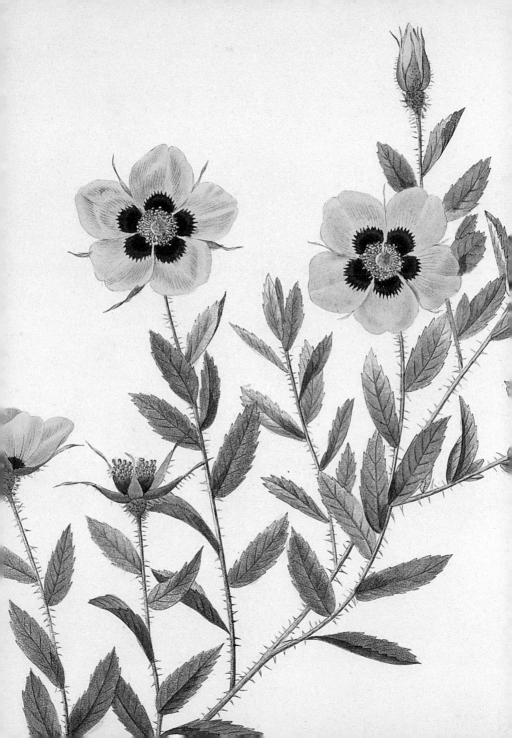

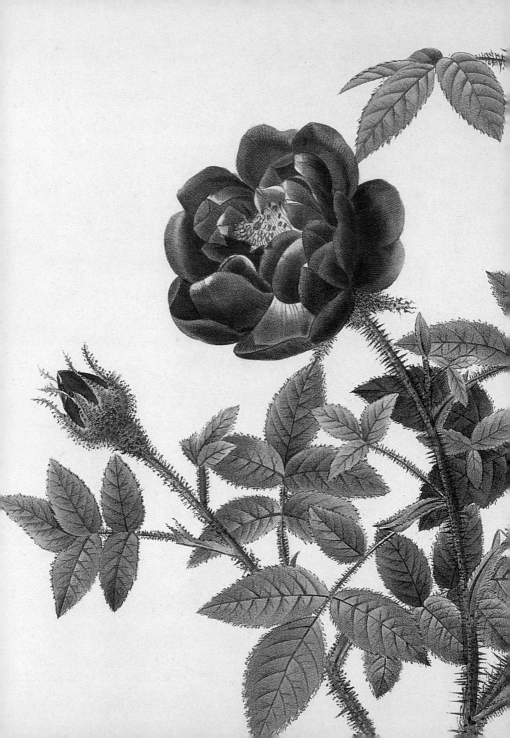

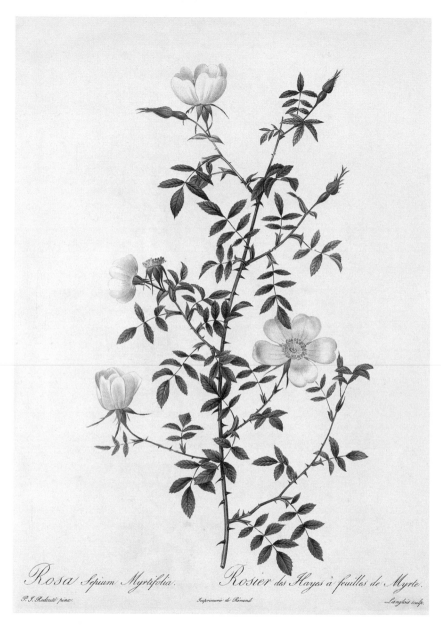

Rosa Sepium Myrtifolia.   *Rosier des Hayes à feuilles de Myrte.*

P. J. Redouté pinx.   Imprimerie de Rémond   Langlois sculp.

ROSA CENTIFOLIA L. VAR. MUSCOSA CV.   ROSA AGRESTIS SAVI
Variety of Moss Rose | Moosrosen-Sorte   Grassland Rose | Ackerrose | Rosier des hayes ⚘
Variété du Rosier mousseux ⚘

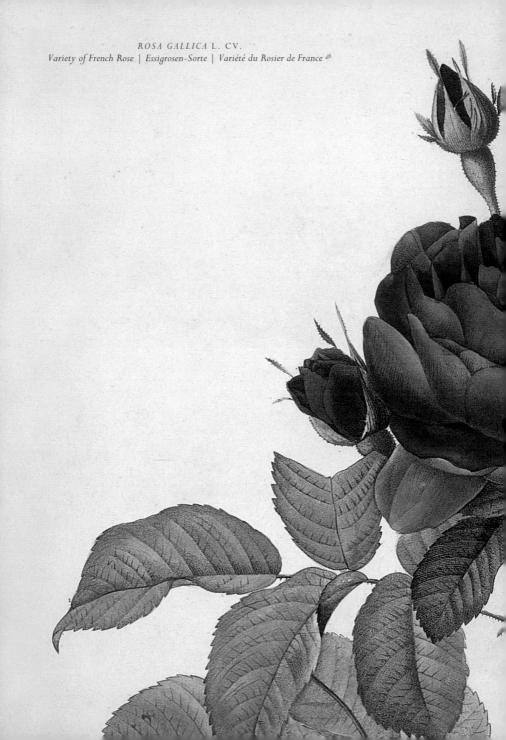

ROSA GALLICA L. CV.

Variety of French Rose | Essigrosen-Sorte | Variété du Rosier de France

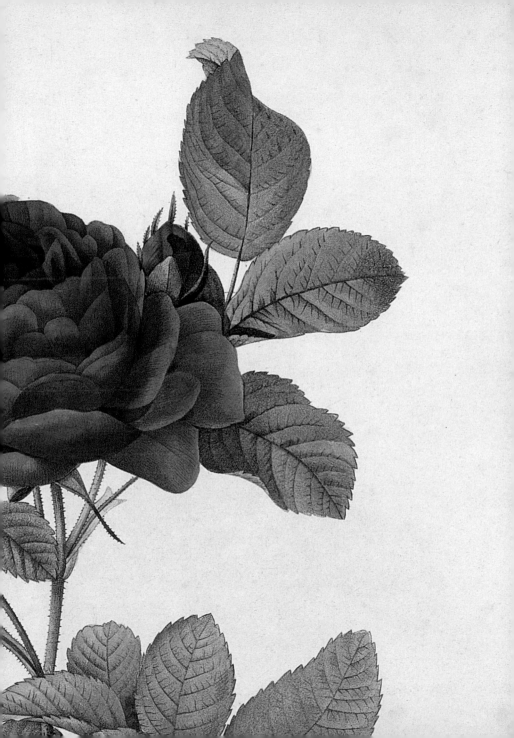

Index

The legends for the illustration plates contain first the botanical term and then popularly used names in English, German and French, if they were able to be determined. The signs at the end refer to the origin: as a wild rose (✿), as garden rose in culture today (❀), not in culture today (✾).

Die Legenden zu den Bildtafeln enthalten jeweils die botanische Bezeichnung sowie die gebräuchlichen Populärnamen in Englisch, Deutsch und Französisch, sofern sie zu ermitteln waren. Die Symbole am Ende verweisen auf das Vorkommen als Wildrose (✿), als Gartenrose in Kultur (❀) und nicht mehr in Kultur (✾).

Les légendes des planches indiquent à chaque fois la désignation botanique ainsi que le nom usuel en anglais, allemand, français, dans la mesure où ils ont pu être établis. Les symboles à la fin ont la signification suivante: rosier sauvage (✿), rosier de jardin en culture (❀) et rosier de jardin n'étant plus en culture (✾).

"Buy them all and add some pleasure to your life."

Art Now
Eds. Burkhard Riemschneider,
Uta Grosenick

Art. The 15th Century
Rose-Marie and Rainer Hagen

Art. The 16th Century
Rose-Marie and Rainer Hagen

Atget's Paris
Ed. Hans Christian Adam

Best of Bizarre
Ed. Eric Kroll

Karl Blossfeldt
Ed. Hans Christian Adam

Chairs
Charlotte & Peter Fiell

Classic Rock Covers
Michael Ochs

Description of Egypt
Ed. Gilles Néret

Design of the 20th Century
Charlotte & Peter Fiell

Dessous
Lingerie as Erotic Weapon
Gilles Néret

Encyclopaedia Anatomica
Museo La Specola Florence

Erotica 17th–18th Century
From Rembrandt to
Fragonard
Gilles Néret

Erotica 19th Century
From Courbet to Gauguin
Gilles Néret

Erotica 20th Century, Vol. I
From Rodin to Picasso
Gilles Néret

Erotica 20th Century, Vol. II
From Dalí to Crumb
Gilles Néret

The Garden at Eichstätt
Basilius Besler

Indian Style
Ed. Angelika Taschen

Male Nudes
David Leddick

Man Ray
Ed. Manfred Heiting

Native Americans
Edward S. Curtis
Ed. Hans Christian Adam

Paris-Hollywood.
Serge Jacques
Ed. Gilles Néret

20th Century Photography
Museum Ludwig Cologne

Pin-Ups
Ed. Burkhard Riemschneider

Giovanni Battista Piranesi
Luigi Ficacci

Provence Style
Ed. Angelika Taschen

Redouté's Roses
Pierre-Joseph Redouté

Robots and Spaceships
Ed. Teruhisa Kitahara

Eric Stanton
Reunion in Ropes & Other
Stories
Ed. Burkhard Riemschneider

Eric Stanton
The Sexorcist & Other Stories
Ed. Burkhard Riemschneider

Tattoos
Ed. Henk Schiffmacher

Edward Weston
Ed. Manfred Heiting

www.taschen.com

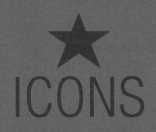